Discover
Britain's
historic
houses

Northwest England

Discover **Britain's**

Published by Reader's Digest Association Ltd
London • New York • Sydney • Montreal

Reader's Digest

Northwest England

historic houses

Simon Jenkins

Contents

2 LANCASHIRE

The best in Britain

WALES

84 Beaumaris Castle
82 Caernarfon Castle
43 Caerphilly Castle
42 Castell Coch
86 Conwy Castle
87 Erddig
85 Plas Mawr
83 Plas Newydd
73 Powis Castle
45 Raglan Castle
44 Tredegar House

ENGLAND

110 Alnwick Castle
62 Althorp
68 Arbury Hall
11 Arundel Castle
95 Astley Hall *
4 Athelhampton House
58 Audley End
15 Bateman's
77 Belton House
75 Belvoir Castle
99 Beningbrough Hall
46 Berkeley Castle
47 Blenheim Palace
81 Blickling Hall
92 Bolsover Castle *
69 Boughton House
12 Brighton Pavilion
55 Broughton Castle *
71 Burghley House
103 Burton Agnes Hall
97 Burton Constable Hall

2 Saltram House
18 Sherborne Castle
105 Sizergh Castle
88 Speke Hall *
39 Spencer House
63 St John's College
33 Syon House
30 The Vyne
64 Trinity College
7 Uppark
49 Waddesdon Manor

108 Wallington Hall
60 Warwick Castle
Wightwick Manor *
67 Wilton House
20 Windsor Castle
31 Windsor Castle
57 Woburn Abbey

Legend

5 Star
4 Star
* Featured in this book

I visited these buildings after writing a book on English churches and the experience was as moving as it was different. While places of worship were built according to the authority and liturgy of the Church, people built houses for themselves. A house was useful first and beautiful second, and from this derives the joy of visiting houses. They are a conversation between utility and beauty down the ages.

In defining the word 'house' I soon found that I could not sensibly distinguish castle from palace, house from hut, roof from ruin. My list embraces any structure in which men and women have laid their heads, provided that they are in some degree accessible to public view. The selection is a personal list and the commentary is a personal vision, warts and all.

Simon Jenkins

Historic houses
of Northwest England

Cheshire is one of England's richest corners. A traditional farming region, it was the commuter belt for Manchester and Liverpool in the 19th century and never looked back. Parts of the county embrace the Peak District and the south and west have rolling contours and exciting rocky outcrops. Apart from the crusader castle at Beeston, the earliest houses are the signature timbered black-and-white halls of the northwest. Bramall and Gawsworth are excellent examples; the 'magpie' house Little Moreton is a feast of medieval carpentry while the hall at Adlington has unique tree-trunk pillars.

The Jacobeans produced the prodigy house at Crewe Hall, and ornate Great Chambers at Combermere and Dorfold. The Georgians came to Cheshire with trumpets blaring at Leoni's Lyme Park, pianissimo at Belmont. The Wyatt dynasty was prolific here, with Samuel and Lewis's masterpiece for the Egertons at Tatton Park and rooms at Dorfold, Lyme, Rode and

Winnington. The Gothic revival was lighthearted at Cholmondeley and in earnest at Peckforton. Most remarkable is the new lease of life given to so many houses through commercial use. Cheshire is exemplary in making old buildings earn their keep.

Derbyshire is a prince among counties. The Peak District was long a land of magnates, but even the coal country saw a phalanx of stately houses which, in their day, might have rivalled the châteaux of the Loire. Haddon Hall is a defining house of the Middle Ages, astonishingly intact. Elizabethan style is nowhere better displayed than in the works associated with Bess of Hardwick: Old Hardwick is derelict but the new hall she built next door is the most complete prodigy house in England. Her Cavendish sons developed Bolsover and Chatsworth. The Little Castle at Bolsover is an exquisite pavilion of 'courtly love', to which William Cavendish added a sumptuous palace.

Then the Vernons built Sudbury, with its rich staircase carving and plasterwork. The brief era of English Baroque includes Calke, Sutton Scarsdale and most of the Chatsworth interiors. To compete with this ostentatious Whiggery, the Tory Curzons had Robert Adam design cold, magnificent Kedleston. In the 19th century, the 6th Duke of Devonshire brought Jeffry Wyatville to help him extend Chatsworth and the Sitwells extended exotic Renishaw.

In the north of **Lancashire**, medieval peles are buried at Borwick and Turton. The county's medieval glory is its black-and-white 'magpie houses' with spectacular timberwork at Smithills, Speke, Rufford, Ordsall, Samlesbury and Wythenshawe. Of no less distinction are the stone courtyards of Stonyhurst and Hoghton and the compact mansion at Gawthorpe. These houses and their successors were mostly those of a recusant gentry, denied preferment, held to their land and starved of the wealth to rebuild. Eccentricities resulted, such as the archaic façade at Astley, contrasted with the novelty of its interior plasterwork. A modest Queen Anne front was applied to Croxteth and a fine Great Hall at Towneley. Yet in the 18th century the gentry went on Grand Tours and returned to commission Carr's Lytham Hall and the great James Wyatt mansion at Heaton. The furniture of the Gillow family of Lancaster is found in most grand houses of the North. Pre-eminent of the big 19th-century houses is Scarisbrick, eccentric Gothic mansion of the Pugins. Others refurbished during the period. Leighton was gothicized, followed by Charles Barry's work at Gawthorpe while the Jacobean revival restored Speke, Samlesbury and Hoghton.

Staffordshire has many gems amid its industrial areas. Buried in a suburb of West Bromwich is the medieval and moated Old Manor House. Ford Green Hall is an outstanding Elizabethan work in outer Stoke. Moseley Old Hall is a delicious reminder of mid-17th-century comfort. Weston Park is one of the few English houses designed by a woman, Lady Wilbraham. Staffordshire shone under the Georgians. Soane gave Chillington one of his most splendid halls. Shugborough is Samuel Wyatt's masterpiece. For architectural landscapes, Staffordshire can hardly be rivalled, with Capability Brown and James Paine at Chillington and Weston, 'Athenian' Stuart at Shugborough, and all and sundry at Alton Towers. The last is one of the most romantic 'ghost' houses in England, built by A. W. N. Pugin for the Earl of Shrewsbury and crying out for rescue from its theme park. The 19th century was crowned by Wightwick, epitome of an erudite Arts and Crafts residence.

✫ STAR RATINGS AND ACCESSIBILITY ✫✫✫✫

The 'star' ratings are entirely my personal choice (but see note below). They rate the overall quality of the house as presented to the public, and not gardens or other attractions. On balance I scaled down houses, however famous, for not being easily accessible or for being only partly open.

The top rating, five stars, is given to those houses that qualify as 'international' celebrities. Four stars are awarded to houses of outstanding architectural quality and public display. Three-star houses comprise the run of good historic houses, well displayed and worthy of national promotion. Two and one-star houses are of more local interest, are hard to visit, or have just one significant feature.

Accessibility varies greatly, from buildings that are open all year to houses that can only be visited 'by appointment' (rarely, I have broken my rule and included a private property that is not open at all, but is viewable from nearby walks or public gardens). Opening hours tend to alter from year to year, but an indication of how accessible a house is to visitors is given at the start of each entry, together with brief information on location and ownership. Many of the houses are National Trust or English Heritage properties, some are now museums or hotels, others are privately owned by families who open to the public for part of the year (English Heritage grant requirements insist on 28 days minimum). Some owners may, understandably, seek to cluster visitors on particular days. More details for each house are given at the back of this book, and readers are advised to check before visiting.

A final note, houses are, or should be, living things subject to constant change and how we view them is bound to be a subject of debate. I welcome any correction or comment, especially from house owners, sent to me c/o the publisher.

NOTE: On the UK map (pages 6-7) the 4 and 5-star houses in England and Wales were selected by Simon Jenkins. Those in Scotland were selected by Hamish Scott and the editors of Reader's Digest.

Architectural timeline
and Northwest England houses in brief

Adlington Hall
A medieval courtyard stands at the heart of the house, with a 15th-century Great Hall. The brick-clad north façade is Restoration; two sides of the quadrangle are Georgian.

Alton Castle
A castle designed by A. W N. Pugin for the 16th Earl of Shrewsbury, it resembles a Rhineland schloss.

Alton Towers
The ruins of a palatial house, built for the Earls of Shrewsbury from 1810. It was taken over in 1837 by A. W. N. Pugin and heavily Gothicized.

Arley Hall
Brick-clad Victorian house in late-Elizabethan style, by George Latham, finished in 1841 with copies of Elizabethan and Jacobean ceilings.

Astley Hall
Elizabethan house altered in the 1660s. The main front has the of look 20th-century neo-Elizabethan architecture.

Barlaston Hall
Palladian villa of 1756 designed by Robert Taylor to a cruciform plan with the main reception rooms set round a central stair case hall, rising to full-height.

Barlborough Hall
Built in 1583 by a prominent Elizabethan judge. Its Renaissance style, symmetrical architecture and similarity to Hardwick Hall have suggested Robert Smythson as architect.

Beeston Castle
Medieval fortress built in 1225 by the Earl of Chester in imitation of the Crusader castles of the Holy Land. The inner bailey on its hill top is enclosed by a massive outer bailey.

Belmont Hall
A Georgian house of the 1750s by James Gibbs, with pedimented façade and two bow windows. The original Rococo-style plasterwork survives inside.

Bolsover Castle
Built by Bess of Hardwick's son and grandson, Bolsover is an English Renaissance palace, designed by the son of Robert Smythson.

Borwick Hall
A house with Great Hall and family wing built in the late 16th century around an existing pele tower.

Bramall Hall
A black-and-white Tudor manor house created around a medieval hall house; Victorian owners kept alterations in keeping.

Browsholme Hall
Of medieval origin, but added to over the centuries. Jeffry Wyatt added two new Regency-style reception rooms in the early 19th century.

Burnley: Towneley Hall
Family home of the Towneleys with an English Baroque Great Hall, decorated with Vassalli plasterwork. Several formal rooms were added by Jeffry Wyatt in the early 19th century.

Calke Abbey
An early 18th-century house, reputedly by Smith of Warwick, built around an Elizabethan courtyard house. It contains the clutter of several centuries-worth of family possessions.

Capesthorne Hall
A monumental Victorian house with many turrets, towers and gables, designed in neo-Jacobean style by Edward Blore; adapted and enhanced by Anthony Salvin in the 1860s.

Carnfield Hall
An Elizabethan manor house with Jacobean wings and a later 17th-century façade. The Hall is home to the owner's personal collection of antiques and curios.

Casterne Hall
An ancient family house, high in the Peaks. The façade appears Queen Anne but dates from the 1730s.

Catton Hall
A red-brick Georgian house begun by James Gibbs and taken on by Smith of Warwick. Inside is fine Rococo plasterwork.

Chatsworth House
Home of the Dukes of Devonshire, rebuilt in the 1690s, when the State rooms were created, and re-made into a palace in the 19th century. The grounds are by Capability Brown.

Chesterfield: Revolution House
Once an inn, the Glorious Revolution of 1688 and the overthrow of the Stuart king, James II, were plotted at this simple country house .

Chillington Hall
Built in two phases in the 18th century; the first part is probably by Richard Trubshaw, the second part was the work of Sir John Soane.

Cholmondeley Castle
A neo-Gothic pseudo castle, designed by the owner, the 1st Marquess of Cholmondeley, with additions by Robert Smirke in 1829.

Clifton Hall
Two apparent early Georgian houses are in fact the wings of a much bigger house, designed by Francis Smith of Warwick.

Combermere Abbey
A Tudor mansion incorporating the original abbey's Great Hall. A Gothick exterior was added in the early 19th century.

Crewe Hall
A Jacobean mansion with Renaissance frontispiece. E.M. Barry rebuilt it in the 1860s after a fire and interiors are by J.G. Crace.

Croxteth Hall
Grand house built around a courtyard. A Queen Anne range stands above a Baroque terrace; the entrance range is Edwardian.

Derby: Pickford's House
A town house with impressive façade built in 1769 by a local architect, Joseph Pickford. Some rooms are presented as if still in use.

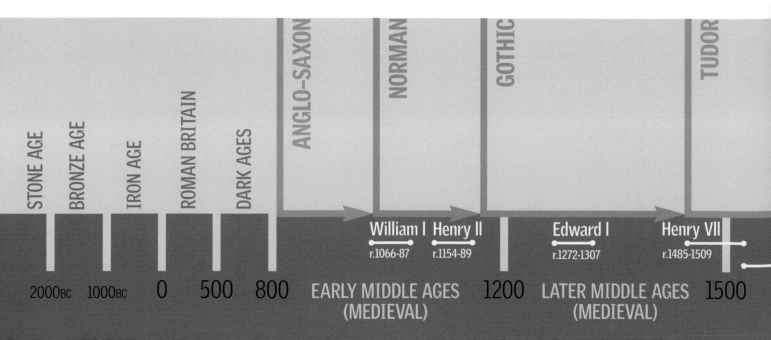

STONE AGE | BRONZE AGE | IRON AGE | ROMAN BRITAIN | DARK AGES | ANGLO-SAXON | NORMAN | GOTHIC | TUDOR

William I r.1066-87   Henry II r.1154-89   Edward I r.1272-1307   Henry VII r.1485-1509

2000BC   1000BC   0   500   800   EARLY MIDDLE AGES (MEDIEVAL)   1200   LATER MIDDLE AGES (MEDIEVAL)   1500

Dorfold Hall
A red-brick Jacobean house, built in 1616, its ground floor altered in the 18th century by William Baker and Samuel Wyatt.

Dunham Massey
A 18th-century house with redbrick exterior and stone centrepiece; its roofline was altered in the early 20th century. Georgian interiors were remodelled by Edwardian owners.

Eyam Hall
Built in the 1670s, in the Elizabethan style. The rooms retain much of their 17th-century appearance, including a superb tapestry room.

Ford Green Hall
A black-and-white, half-timbered house built for a yeoman farmer in 1624. A new wing was added in 1734.

Gawsworth Hall
A typical Cheshire black-and-white 'magpie' house, built round a three-sided courtyard and much restored. In the grounds are the remains of a Tudor tilting ground.

Gawthorpe Hall
A late Elizabethan mansion, possibly designed by Robert Smythson and probably built around a pele, which became the staircase tower. Sir Charles Barry restored the house in 1849.

Haddon Hall
A medieval fortified house, enclosed within a curtain wall and built around a courtyard. The Great Hall dates from the 1370s while the solar wing is 15th century.

Haigh Hall
Classical mansion built in the 19th century set in a landscaped park laid out in the 1860s. The house was made using locally sourced stone, ironwork and wood.

Hall i' th' Wood
A black-and-white timber-framed house built in the late 15th century and extended in the 1640s. Once the home of Samuel Crompton it was restored by Lord Leverhulme.

Hardwick Hall
The archetypal Elizabethan Renaissance house, designed to celebrate the importance of its owner, it was built for the formidable Bess of Hardwick, probably by Robert Smythson.

Black-and-white 'magpie' houses

The timber-framed buildings of the Northwest of England are often called 'magpie' houses in a clear reference to their stark colours. What marks out these houses in Cheshire, Lancashire and parts of the Midlands is the extent to which the timbers are arranged in a decorative effect.

In historically-forested Britain, wood was the building material of choice from earliest times. Stone was used for the homes of only the wealthiest builders. Even brick, before mass production was a luxury material. So vernacular architecture was based on a timber structure for centuries.

In a traditional half-timbered building the load-bearing structure was made up of vertical and horizontal posts and beams, often supported by diagonal trusses and braces. A framework was created between these timbers with subsidiary supports – upright studs, horizontal noggin pieces and diagonal herringbone braces. The frame was then filled in – maybe with wattle and daub or rubble – and plastered over, leaving the timbers visible both inside and out. The builders of 'magpie' houses used the timbers to create geometric patterns within the framework.

Hardwick Old Hall
The birthplace of Bess of Hardwick, extended by her while she built the new Hall. It had important state chambers on the upper floors.

Heaton Hall
Georgian villa of 1772 by James Wyatt. The interiors were decorated by craftsmen who had collaborated with Adam on other projects.

Highfields
An Elizabethan manor house, it was stuccoed by Victorian owners but original black-and-white façade has been revealed once more.

Hoar Cross Hall
A neo-Jacobean house designed by Henry Clutton in the late 19th century. Inside are plasterwork ceilings by architect G. F. Bodley and wallpapers by William Morris.

Hoghton Tower
Elizabethan house built around two courtyards. The interiors were restored in the 19th century by Paley & Austin.

Ince Blundell
Early Georgian house designed by Henry Sephton of Liverpool, c1720 for Robert Blundell. His son added to the house in order to accommodate his collection of sculpture.

Izaak Walton's Cottage
A half-timbered farmhouse cottage, roofed with thatch, bought by Izaak Walton, author of The Compleat Angler, in 1655 to benefit the local poor.

Kedleston Hall
Begun in Palladian style by Matthew Brettingham and James Paine, but finished by Robert Adam in Roman style.

Kinver Rock Houses
Cave houses cut into the sandstone of Kinver Edge; the upper caves were fronted by a brick house but the lower ones have been restored.

Lancaster: Cottage Museum
An 18th-century, or earlier, cottage in the heart of the city. Preserved as a cloth-working family home of 1820–50 and sparsely furnished.

Lancaster: Judges' Lodgings
Late 17th-century town house, near Lancaster castle. Once the lodgings of local Circuit judges, it was the home, in earlier times, of the castle Keeper. Furnished with pieces by Gillow.

Leighton Hall
A mid-18th-century house bought by the Gillow family in the 1820s, who gave it a Gothick exterior and hallway. The interior has fine furniture made by the family firm.

Lichfield: Erasmus Darwin House
Home of Erasmus Darwin, scientist, writer and grandfather of Charles Darwin. Built in the 1760s onto an existing medieval house; the façade is graced with four Venetian windows.

Lichfield: Johnson's Birthplace
The childhood home of Dr Johnson, built in 1707: the house's top two storeys jetty out over the ground floor, supported by columns.

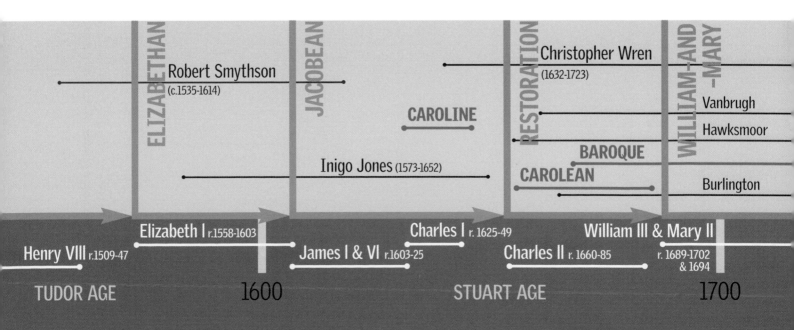

ELIZABETHAN
Robert Smythson (c.1535-1614)

JACOBEAN

RESTORATION

Christopher Wren (1632-1723)

WILLIAM-AND-MARY

CAROLINE

Vanbrugh

Hawksmoor

BAROQUE

Inigo Jones (1573-1652)

CAROLEAN

Burlington

Elizabeth I r.1558-1603

Charles I r.1625-49

William III & Mary II

Henry VIII r.1509-47

James I & VI r.1603-25

Charles II r.1660-85

r.1689-1702 & 1694

TUDOR AGE

1600

STUART AGE

1700

Robert Adam (1728–92)

The most successful scion of an architectural dynasty, Robert Adam and his brothers, James and John, trained in the Edinburgh office of their father, William Adam, the leading architect of Georgian Scotland. Even before his Grand Tour of Rome in 1754, Robert had completed a commission for Dumfries House, In Rome, he studied the classical architecture that had such an influence on his later work.

On his return in 1758, Kedleston Hall (see page 86) was one of his first buildings; the drawings he had made in Rome helped secure the patronage of Lord Curzon. He would work on some of Britain's greatest stately homes, including Syon House, Osterley Park and Kenwood House.

Adam's skill lay in adapting the architectural motifs of ancient Rome into a classicism that was lighter and more imaginative than the Palladianism of the early 18th century. Although the exteriors of his buildings reflect these innovations, it is his interiors that best show the originality and effectiveness of the 'Adam style'. His rooms combined painting, plasterwork and architectural motifs to create a cohesive scheme of decoration.

Little Moreton Hall
A classic 'magpie' house, built in the 1450s around a courtyard with gatehouse and Great Hall. It was extended in the 16th century with the Long Gallery added in the 1580s.

Liverpool: Lennon House
A 1930s semi-detached house in the suburbs of Liverpool, once home to John Lennon and restored in 1950s style.

Liverpool: McCartney House
A Liverpool council house designed by the City architect, Sir Lancelot Keay in the 1950s. It became the home of Paul McCartney in 1955.

Liverpool: Sudley House
The home of a Liverpool shipping magnate, built from local red sandstone in the 1830s in a Greek revival style. It houses the Holt collection of 18th- and 19th-century art.

Lyme Park
An Elizabethan house on the site of an earlier hunting lodge, it was transformed into a Palladian palace by Giacomo Leoni.

Lytham Hall
A Georgian mansion made of red brick and white dressings, designed by Carr of York in 1757 with a Baroque staircase hall.

Martholme
The remains of a medieval hall house, the service wing and screens passage survive, with the interiors of the buttery and pantry intact.

Melbourne Hall
A 17th-century house extended in the 18th; William Smith of Warwick added a wing in 1744. The dining room was the Jacobean Great Hall; the current hall is part of the Georgian building.

Meols Hall
A 20th-century house built as a suitable seat for an ancient family and as a home for a painting collection. Designed in neo-Georgian style and built in the 1960s.

Moseley Old Hall
Here, Charles II sought refuge after defeat at the Battle of Worcester. Originally a black-and-white building, the house was clad with a red-brick exterior during the 19th century.

Peckforton Castle
A Victorian castle, built as a home for Lord Tollemache by Anthony Salvin in 1844. It stands high on a rock, enjoying a prominent position overlooking the Cheshire plain.

Peover Hall
An Elizabethan manor house that once had a Georgian wing, replaced in the 1960s with an Elizabethan-style brick-built range. The stable are the most architecturally important feature.

Quarry Bank Mill: The Apprentice House
Built as accommodation for apprentices in the nearby cotton mill. Children were given food shelter, and clothing, and some education.

Renishaw Hall
A house built in the 1620s and given Gothick additions some 200 years later. Inside, some Jacobean interiors remain while others are decorated in Georgian and Regency style.

Rode Hall
A red-brick house of two parts; an earlier, Queen-Anne range is attached to a mid-Georgian, three-storey house.

Rufford Old Hall
An important 'magpie' house, built around a Tudor Great Hall, originally to an H-plan. The hall has a unique movable screen.

Salford: Ordsall Hall
A house with a 15th-century, black-and-white Hall, its timber frame displaying a quatrefoil pattern. Two large, full-length window bays project into the courtyard.

Samlesbury Hall
A Great Hall and one wing survive from a 15th-century black-and-white house, decorated with herringbone and quatrefoil patterns. Heavily restored in the 19th century.

Sandon Hall
Built in 1852 to a neo-Jacobean design by William Burn, yhe symmetrical E-plan façade is dominated by the central bay, topped by turrets and with a large porte-cochère.

Scarisbrick Hall
A Victorian Gothic pile, started by Thomas Rickman. The project was taken over by A.W.N. Pugin but left unfinished on his death. His son, E.W. Pugin, took over the commission.

Shugborough
A William-and-Mary house extended in the 1740s and transformed by Samuel Wyatt who between 1790 and 1806 gave the façade a grand colonnade, flanked by two new wings.

Sinai House
A medieval moated house, extended during the Tudor era, that fell into ruin during the 20th century. One wing has been rebuilt and includes fragments of surviving wall paintings.

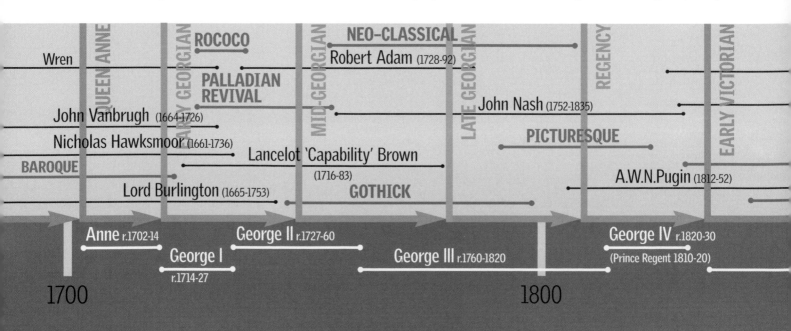

Smithills Hall
A medieval hall house from the 14th century, added to in the 16th and 19th centuries. The Victorian wing was inspired by William Morris.

Speke Hall
A black-and-white Elizabethan moated mansion of four wings around a courtyard. The original interiors remain.

Stafford: Ancient High House
A black-and-white town house, rebuilt in the late 16th century. The number of windows and chimneys, and the decorative timbering reflect the wealth of the original owner.

Stonyhurst
A grand Elizabethan house, begun in 1592 but left unfinished. Passed to the Jesuits for use as a school in the late 18th century; further additions in the 19th century include a chapel.

Sudbury Hall
A Restoration-era house, built in Jacobean, style. The interiors are finished with the most fashionable decoration of the time.

Sutton Scarsdale Hall
A mansion built in 1724 by Francis Smith of Warwick, once decorated with plasterwork by Artari and Vassalli; now a ruined shell.

Tabley House
A grand Palladian mansion, designed by Carr of York in 1761. On the south front, double curving stairs lead to an impressive portico.

Tamworth Castle
A Norman motte-and-bailey castle; the shell keep remains. The interiors reflect the long history of the castle's occupation, from the Middle Ages to the late 19th century.

Tatton Old Hall
A late medieval hall house, converted in Tudor times and clad with a brick façade.

Tatton Park
A house begun in 1716 but then refashioned by Samuel and Lewis Wyatt in neo-classical style in the 1780s. A modest Palladian façade conceals a grand and extensive mansion.

Tissington Hall
Jacobean house of 1609, with hall arranged front to back and main reception rooms set on the first floor. It has an Edwardian library.

Prodigy houses

The Elizabethan era was a time of great wealth for the nation's elite. No longer tied by obligations to the Church, many of the ruling class chose to display their status by building on a grand scale. Their palatial new homes came to be known as prodigy houses.

Designed to impress, these houses were often built by courtiers who hoped to attract a visit from the Queen. They had to be large enough to accommodate the royal entourage and be spectacular enough to act as a backdrop for lavish ceremonies and entertainments.

Prodigy houses rose to new heights, extending upward to three or more storeys, with the grandest formal chambers set on the upper floors. The E-plan appeared, with projecting wings and elaborate central porch; symmetry became the essential rule in architecture. The finest prodigy houses also included the newest innovations in building technology; improvements in heating methods led to an increase in fireplaces and flues and the roofs of houses like Burghley and Longleat were a forest of chimneys. Glass was expensive so the more windows there were, the wealthier the owner; Hardwick Hall (see page 79), so the saying went, was 'more glass than wall'. The internal decoration had to be of the highest quality and reflect the tastes and sensibilities of the day, taking the Italian Renaissance as its inspiration.

Trentham Park
The entrance colonnade and porte-cochère of an Italianate house, are all that remain of a mansion, designed by Sir Charles Barry in the 1830s, with grounds by William Nesfield.

Turton Tower
A 15th-century pele tower, once partnered by a neighbouring cruck house. The latter was enclosed by a 19th-century black-and-white building that joined onto the pele tower.

West Bromwich: Oak House
A black-and-white manor house from the turn of the 17th century. The gabled façade is three bays wide, with a gabled porch off centre.

West Bromwich: Old Manor House
A complete medieval moated manor house, dating back to the late 13th century. An Elizabethan gatehouse leads to the medieval courtyard; the solar wing and chapel survive.

Weston Park
House built in 1671, possibly designed by the owner, Lady Wilbraham, influenced by Palladian principles. The original central courtyard was enclosed in the 19th century.

Whitmore Hall
A medieval timbered house that was enclosed in brick in 1676 and then given a new façade in the 18th century. Nearby is an Elizabethan stable block with early 17th-century stalls.

Wightwick Manor
A Victorian house built in the Tudor style and designed by Edward Ould. The owners were influenced by the aesthetics of the Arts-and-Crafts movement and furnished the house accordingly.

Wingfield Manor
The ruined remains of a 15th-century palace built by Ralph Cromwell, then the richest man in England. The remnants of the grand formal rooms can still be seen.

Winnington Hall
A stone mansion designed in the 1780s by Samuel Wyatt with a black-and-white wing, a Victorianized 17th-century building. It was the home of the founders of ICI in the late 19th century.

Wolverhampton: Bantock House
A Georgian house with late Victorian interiors, owned by a prominent Wolverhampton family who chose to decorated their home in the Arts-and-Crafts style.

Wythenshawe Hall
A Tudor house with medieval core and Victorian additions. Inside are surviving Tudor and Elizabethan interiors, including fragments of original wall paintings.

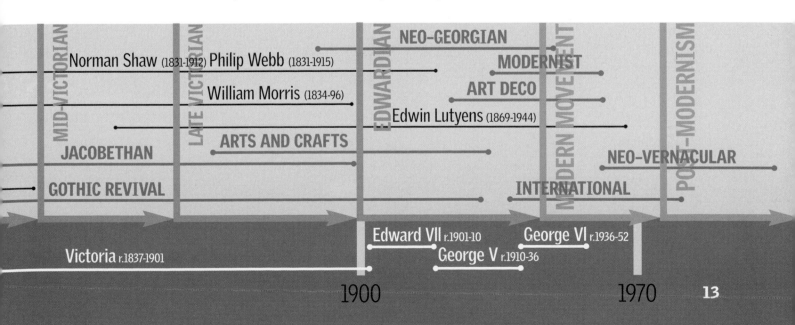

MID-VICTORIAN

LATE VICTORIAN

EDWARDIAN

MODERN MOVEMENT

POST-MODERNISM

NEO-GEORGIAN

Norman Shaw (1831-1912) Philip Webb (1831-1915)

MODERNIST

William Morris (1834-96)

ART DECO

Edwin Lutyens (1869-1944)

ARTS AND CRAFTS

JACOBETHAN

NEO-VERNACULAR

GOTHIC REVIVAL

INTERNATIONAL

MODERNISM

Edward VII r.1901-10   George VI r.1936-52

George V r.1910-36

Victoria r.1837-1901

1900

1970

Beeston Castle

Cheshire

Adlington hall

★ ★ ★ A medieval Cheshire house with many later additions

5 miles N of Macclesfield; private house, open part year

Left The magnificent organ in the medieval Great Hall at Adlington was inserted between the two carved oak-tree pillars that support the hall in around 1670. Bernard Smith (Schmidt), its designer, was the most renowned organ builder of his day. Smith, who made organs for Westminster Abbey, Durham Cathedral and St Paul's, originally came from Halle, the birthplace of Handel, who visited Adlington in 1751.

'the Hall ... is supported ... by **two giant oak trunks.'**

Adlington is a place of all periods and moods. It is part Cheshire black-and-white, part Tudor brick, part Restoration and part 18th century. The house has been owned by a branch of the Cheshire Legh family since the Middle Ages. In cases of female succession, husbands have been expected to become Leghs; a recent owner, Charles Legh, was son of Cynthia Legh and Ralph Broughton. The present owner is his daughter Mrs Camilla Legh.

The core is four-sided medieval courtyard, with a 15th-century Great Hall and surrounding wings built in the late 16th century. The north front behind the hall was refaced and refenestrated in brick after the Restoration, to present a handsome gabled façade. Then, in the 1740s and 1750s, Charles Legh decided to demolish the two south sides of the quadrangle and rebuild them in the Georgian style. The exterior of this wing, formally the front of the house, demonstrates the waywardness of 18th-century design. The portico is most odd, built to balance a wider façade and heightened by elongated bases. A walk around the outside and courtyard of Adlington is a historical tableau of English architecture.

The old Great Hall is one of the most remarkable in England. The passage and gallery are supported, as is the Hall, by two giant oak trunks. They are dead but their roots are still deep in the ground. The uprights have been carved to octagonal shape and covered with panels. They lean towards the hammerbeam roof of *c*1480. Between the trees is a Baroque gallery and late 17th-century organ designed by Bernard Smith. It is one of the largest of its date in the country and would (surely) have been played by Handel when staying at Adlington. With trumpeting cherubs in the celure above and murals of musical saints on either side, the organ marries nature and music.

The rest of the Great Hall is either window or mural. The colourful west end is formed of a huge coved canopy with 60 panels of Cheshire heraldry. Beneath is a wall painting of Hector and Andromache. Sixteenth-century murals depicting the history of Troy cover the side walls. They were hidden until 1859 when a member of the family playing shuttlecock dislodged the plaster and revealed paint beneath.

On the other side of the screens passage is a Carolean staircase, with chunky twisted balusters and pineapple finials. It leads to a suite of rooms along the 17th-century north front, all panelled and with robust Restoration furniture.

Arley hall

★★ Grand Jacobethan house of typical Victorian squire

At Arley, 6 miles N of Northwich; private house, open part year

Arley has been home of the Warburtons, Viscounts Ashbrook, since the Norman Conquest. It lies in a precious enclave of green just a mile from the M6. The Georgian Sir Peter Warburton encased the medieval house in brick and stucco. His firm countenance and bushy eyebrows are captured by William Beechey in a portrait of 1811 which hangs in the house. He was of the old school and expected his house to be likewise. A footman complained that it was in such a poor state that his powdered hair was nibbled away one night by rats.

Dying without issue in 1813, Sir Peter settled his estate on his eight-year-old great-nephew, Rowland Egerton, who adopted his benefactor's name. Rowland grew to become a model Victorian squire, 'a good churchman, a good landlord, a keen sportsman and a man of literary tastes'. When at the age of twenty-six he courted and then became engaged to a local girl, Mary Brooke, she wrote that 'I am to be married to Mr Warburton! The very last person I have thought would have got so soon into this scrape.' The couple immediately set about building a new house and garden.

Rowland Egerton-Warburton typified the change that overcame the English countryside and English taste in the 19th century. His reign at Arley lasted until 1891, his interests embracing everything from Anglo-Catholicism to the workers' cottages on his estate. Like many of his age, in selecting a design for his house, he wished to avoid the formality of classicism, preferring medieval piety with a touch of Elizabethan grandeur. And nothing should be too expensive.

George Latham, a local architect, was apparently the man. He promised a grand house for no more than £6,000. After much argument over what features were strictly 'Elizabethan', the final cost was £30,000. The outside, completed in 1841, is a dignified late Elizabethan façade of diapered brickwork, Dutch gables, stone windows and a classical porch. The interiors are variations on the same theme. Most remarkable are the ceilings, careful re-creations of 16th- or 17th-century originals. Everywhere the eye is drawn upwards to what Latham assured Warburton were 'the best ceilings of their style in England'.

Arley is a place of ceilings and fireplaces. Plain panelling in the dining room sets the tone for plain early portraits. The library is more exuberant, with caryatids and niches above the fireplace and an elaborate ceiling with frieze and pendants. The gallery ceiling has been repainted in Wedgwood colours.

Arley has reputedly the earliest herbaceous garden in England, and is much loved. Gertrude Jekyll admired it as 'the best kind of English garden of the formal type'.

Below Above the library is one of George Latham's best ceilings at Arley; designed in 1862 and costing £274, it was the work of John Crowther & Sons of Manchester. A London firm, H. Wood & Co of Covent Garden, made the bookcases and chimneypiece in 1843 for the sum of £520.

Beeston castle

★ Castle built like a crusader fortress on a Cheshire crag

At Beeston, 11 miles SE of Chester; English Heritage, open all year

Beeston and Peckforton are the twin glories of the Cheshire plain. They sit atop rocky outcrops and glare at each other. If Peckforton is a Rhineland *schloss*, Beeston is Crac de Chevaliers, a crusader fortress on a bare crag 500 ft above the plain. There are few more dramatic ruins in England.

Beeston was built by Ranulf, Earl of Chester, in 1225 after his return from the Fifth Crusade. Although his base was Chester, he wanted a fortress to display his strength elsewhere in the county. He must also have yearned for a testament of his crusader heroics, employing the new engineering seen in the Levant, cradle of castle architecture. Beeston is thus a true Levantine import, with strong baileys guarded by gatehouses and wall towers rather than a single central keep.

The outer bailey encloses much of the hillside with a series of walls and fortress towers. At the top of the hill is a dramatic ditch and bridge to the inner bailey. This appears never to have been completed as a residence, except for the rooms in the gatehouse itself. Most of the house would have been in the Outer Bailey. On Ranulf's death, the castle was taken by Henry III and used as a fort and storehouse against the Welsh. It fell into disuse but was seized, fortified and defended by the Royalists in the Civil War. After its subsequent slighting, it degenerated into a ruin until rescued as 'picturesque' by Lord Tollemache to improve his view across the valley from Peckforton.

Belmont hall

At Great Budworth, 3 miles N of Northwich; private house, open for tours by arrangement

There are said to be 'as many Leghs as fleas' in Cheshire. The Belmont Leighs (or Leghs) may not have been as rich as those of Lyme Park, but at least they still own the place, albeit now rented to a school. The family live in the stables. The house was designed by James Gibbs c1750 for a scion of neighbouring Marbury, John Smith Barry, as a 'very Convenient Small house'. Belmont is externally plain, with pediment and bow windows.

The chief feature of the house is that Gibbs' forte, plasterwork. The central hall has a Rococo ceiling and a heavier Baroque fireplace. The drawing room walls, fighting against a rising tide of schoolwork, have panels draped in fronds and swags. Over the mantelpiece is the most extraordinary decoration I have encountered in any English house, a pair of knickers belonging to the singer, Cher, mounted in a frame. Are they a teaching aid?

The loveliest plasterwork is on the staircase, where there is an exquisite Rococo trophy of hunting horns below a medallion. The study has a foliage frieze looking out onto the rather bleak garden. The house is full of surprises, such as its beautifully crafted door-plates. It craves a return to family occupation.

Right Belmont Hall is one of James Gibbs' later designs and, like most of the architect's buildings, its interiors are adorned with fine plasterwork decoration.

Bramall hall

★★☆ Medieval black-and-white manor with Victorian additions

3 miles S of Stockport; museum, open part year

Bramall is my favourite among Cheshire's black-and-white houses, despite its burial in Stockport's stockbroker belt. The house belonged to the Davenport family from the time of its 16th-century construction until 1881. Two years later the medieval façade was 'enhanced' by a wealthy calico printer, Charles Nevill, an enthusiastic antiquarian. The encroachment of Stockport led to ever more land being sold for villas and the house eventually passed to the council in 1935. The hall is in excellent condition. Its ballroom is the most enjoyable medieval chamber in the county.

The main front of Bramall is a profusion of Cheshire fenestration. An earlier hall house was converted in the 1590s and given expanses of glass. The plan remains medieval, with an entrance to one side of the Great Hall, solar wing to the right and service quarters to the left. The new first floor is almost all window, so much so that one wonders how the roof was supported, especially as there was once a gallery on top. The present roof gables and much of the surface woodwork are late Victorian, a repeat on the entrance front of the rear façade to the garden.

'... Bramall is a **profusion** of Cheshire **fenestration.**'

Left Paintings on the walls of the ballroom at Bramall Hall were revealed in 1887 when panelling that lined the room was removed. The decoration on the lower walls date from the early 16th century and includes paintings of real and fanciful creatures, set among scrolling foliage. Two 16th-century musicians are painted above the door in the east wall. Plainer, less colourful decoration on the upper parts of the walls dates from the early 17th century.

The Great Hall was divided horizontally at the time of the 1590s modernization and has a 19th-century ceiling. It retains a Tudor pendant in its bay window. Stone felon heads on either side of the fireplace recall the Davenport sinecure of Sergeant of the Forest of Macclesfield. The banqueting room contains painted black-and-white 'timbering effect' introduced by Nevill. A huge painting of a Viking meeting a Saxon on the far wall illustrates the joint heritage of the English race. The artist is Herbert Schmalz, whose name became a byword for such contrived sentimentality.

Above the banqueting room is the ballroom, converted from the pre-Elizabethan solar wing. The magnificent oak roof is cruck-framed with quatrefoil wind-braces. The crucks have beautifully decorated spandrels. The walls were formerly covered in paintings, long hidden behind panelling but revealed by Nevill in the 1880s. Those on the east wall depict musicians in 16th-century dress. Others are cruder, including a hunter being savaged by a boar. Behind the ballroom is Nevill's Room, Elizabethan again merging into Victorian. This is a lovely chamber, with lozenge-glazed windows filtering light over dark panelling. A billiard table waits idly at one end.

Capesthorne hall

✫ ✫ Jacobean-style Victorian pile and home of ancient Cheshire family

Near Siddington, 5 miles W of Macclesfield: private house, open part year

Capesthorne has been the home of the Cheshire squirearchs, the Bromley-Davenports and their ancestors since the Conquest. The enormous house cuts a dash from a distance. The forest of turrets, wings, heraldry, brick and stone are the embodiment of the phrase, 'North Country pile'. Lenette Bromley-Davenport, American mother of the present owner, wrote in 1955 that Capesthorne 'can repel violently or attract irrevocably. To many the exotic towers, domes, and pinnacles are grotesque and ugly.' Yet when the light is right 'the enchantment of Eastern minarets, the tales of Arabian Nights and the romance of the Round Table trembles in the air'.

Although first built in the 18th century by the Smiths of Warwick, the house is to outward appearance mid-19th century, a ponderous neo-Jacobean work of 1837 by Edward Blore. After a fire in 1861, the more talented Anthony Salvin converted Blore's three storeys into two, raising the heights of the main rooms but making them absurdly grand. Lizzie Bromley-Davenport, Lenette's daughter-in-law and a professional artist, confronted

this challenge head on. She simply wallowed the rooms in colour, which is what the Jacobeans would have done. The result is an acquired taste, but successful.

Blore's entrance hall is now a vivid yellow. Its massive chimneypiece carries Flemish figures brought from the chapel. The heraldic glass is by Willement, celebrant of lineage to the Victorian aristocracy. Indeed, the halls and galleries at Capesthorne carry a quantity of family portraiture and sculpture remarkable even for an old English family. The main reception rooms are saved from elephantine tedium by Salvin's flair for decoration and by Lizzie Bromley-Davenport's paintbrush. Most magnificent is Salvin's great saloon, which I saw resplendent for one of the weddings that are key to Capesthorne's financial rebirth. The squires of Capesthorne look down with approval from the walls.

An iron balustrade on the staircase has a cartoon depicting Gladstone as a felon with a rope round his neck. Bromley-Davenports were never Liberals. Upstairs, an American Room commemorates Lenette's Pennsylvania background, its contents rustic and simple compared with the bombast outside.

Cholmondeley castle

★ Castellated mansion in spectacular parkland

7 miles N of Whitchurch; private house, garden open part year

The 1st Marquess of Cholmondeley (pronounced Chumley) decided, in 1801, to demolish an old house by William Smith of Warwick and try to do something better himself. He also owned Houghton, in Norfolk, but Cholmondeley had been the family seat (and name) since the 12th century. His self-designed neo-Gothic house was augmented in 1829 by Robert Smirke, practised supplier of castles to the discerning nobility, with examples at Eastnor, in Herefordshire, and Lowther, in Cumbria. The pile of forbidding pink-grey stone stands on an eminence overlooking its park. It has only two or three storeys, although from below it looks like ten.

Apart from a basement shop, the house is closed to the public, 'but you may get as close as you like,' said a warden, 'and stroke its very walls.' The castle, however, forms the centrepiece of one of the finest and least-known ornamental parks in the North-West. It is the work of the present Dowager Lady Cholmondeley and her late husband in half a century of labour.

Visitors drive down an avenue of chestnuts past spreading lakes to park below the house in a meadow by one of England's loveliest cricket fields. Each tree – cedar, fir, oak, weeping beech – seems to have been sited with care. Perhaps it was the sunshine on my visit, but castle, trees, grass and vista seemed in peculiar harmony. The castle is guarded by a camellia walk. The famous Cholmondeley iron gates, designed in the early 18th century by the Davies firm of Wrexham, are next to the tea-room north of the castle. In the grounds is a charming chapel with Laudian fittings.

Combermere abbey

⋆⋆ Medieval and Tudor house with Gothick exterior

4 miles NE of Whitchurch; private house, open for tours by arrangement

The abbey was a Cistercian house handed to one of Henry VIII's courtiers, Sir George Cotton, at the Dissolution. It was rebuilt as a black-and-white mansion incorporating the former abbot's hall. Cottons lived and prospered at Combermere, acquiring a viscountcy in 1827. The house was sold in 1919. The present owner, Sarah Callander Beckett, was a public relations official for Laura Ashley in New York when she discovered she had inherited the property in 1990. She thought long and hard and rose to the challenge, even asking the local public what they thought she should do with it. The Georgian stables have been converted into holiday cottages. The garden, including reputedly the largest private lake in the country, is being restored. A fine house is returning to life.

Combermere is sited on a rise overlooking its lake. The exterior is the Gothick shell built over a medieval and Tudor interior by Sir Stapleton Cotton in 1814–21. The windows have cusped tracery

'A fine house is **returning to life.**'

Above The library at Combermere occupies the upper part of the original Great Hall; a 17th-century ceiling conceals the hall's original hammerbeam roof. Among the decorative elements here are coats of arms, charting 400 years of Cotton family history. Sir Stapleton Cotton, who rebuilt the exterior of Combermere, can be seen in a painting in the library that commemorates his role in the Peninsular Wars.

and the roof is battlemented. The best work is the out-house courtyard with a clock-tower, and a game larder designed like a Temple of the Winds.

The interior is different, light hearted and domestic. The entrance, hung with Cotton big-game trophies, leads into the Porter's Hall, a gothicized version of the Abbot's Great Hall. On the stairs is a Tillemans painting of the house in its Tudor form. The upper landing is adorned with a magnificent screen, richly panelled on both sides. It appears to be a composite of woodwork from other parts of the house, installed when the hall was divided in 1563.

The upper part of the old Great Hall, now the library, is a room of great decorative force, with strapwork ceiling, heraldic frieze and carved fireplace. Shields and Tudor portraits, coats of arms and grotesques cover every inch. Filling one wall is a huge painting of Sir Stapleton Cotton, one of Wellington's generals, accepting the French defeat under the walls of Salamanca.

Crewe hall

★ ★ ★ Jacobean prodigy house with extraordinary Victorian interiors

2 miles SE of Crewe; now a hotel

My enthusiasm for this building is partly born of relief. What was the wreck of one of the most celebrated Jacobean mansions in England has been taken in hand by a hotel company and its restoration of the Jacobethan interior is masterful. Crewe was built for lavish hospitality and that is what it now offers, although the grounds are surrounded by industrial sprawl.

Sir Randulph Crewe was Lord Chief Justice under James I and built the core of the present house between 1615 and 1639. The family continued in residence until the 1930s, when it passed to the Duchy of Lancaster who used it as a prison for 2,000 German officers during the Second World War. After service as offices, it was left empty until acquired by the hotel in 1998. The Duchy had stripped the building to its bare walls.

The old house is represented by the symmetrical brick entrance front, with Renaissance frontispiece and gabled wings. This house was gutted by fire in 1866 and rebuilt by E. M. Barry. He added a wing and lofty tower to one side. The ensemble is set on a balustraded platform adorned with heraldic beasts.

'Crewe was built **for lavish hospitality...**'

The interior is exuberant Victorian, Jacobean in inspiration and decorated by J. G. Crace at his most flamboyant. The copious stained glass is by Clayton & Bell. The style is mostly Flemish Renaissance, with flourishes of Pre-Raphaelite and Artisan Mannerist revival, a vivid hotch-potch.

The old Great Hall is to the right of the entrance, behind an overblown Mannerist screen. The large Jacobean overmantel is a relief of Plenty, a splendid, apparently 17th-century, work. Beyond, Barry converted the courtyard of the Jacobean house into a covered *cortile*, with cloister below, balcony above and hammerbeam roof on top. The whole space is richly dark, full of towering alabaster chimneypieces and mysterious corners.

The stairs to the main reception rooms pass heraldic beasts, lions, leopards and unicorns, with landings darting into stained-glass alcoves and canopies. Upstairs are the library, drawing room and Long Gallery. Carved alabaster panels depict scenes from English history. Busts portray English literary worthies. Shelves have been restocked with books and walls with paintings. Ceilings are heavy with coffering or riotous strapwork.

Buried beneath the stairs is the Carved Room, a virtuoso Jacobean interior, apparently a facsimile of the original room on this site. Alabaster medallions in deep relief depict the Virtues of which Crewes should be proud. Over the fireplace is a relief of Father Time, with two boys portraying Industry and Idleness. Not an inch is without decoration.

The restored chapel is full of coloured alabaster and marble, with Pre-Raphaelite paintings and glass. A glorious revival.

Above E. M. Barry, like his father Sir Charles, was able to adapt the architecture of an earlier age to his designs; at Crewe Hall, the staircase is executed in Jacobean style. After his father's death, E. M. Barry completed the Houses of Parliament, Sir Charles' Victorian-Gothic masterpiece.

Dorfold hall

★ ★ Jacobean house with Georgian alterations

At Acton, 1½ miles W of Nantwich; private house, open part year

How tastes change! The present lovely lime avenue and courtyard of Dorfold Hall were designed in 1862 as a birthday surprise for the lady of the house while she was away on holiday. She was so outraged by what her husband had done that she refused to speak to him for six months. Today, Dorfold looks delightful, a vista of gables, chimneys and finials enclosed by a stone balustrade and gateposts. The brick is dark Cheshire red, with stone dressings. The flanking outhouses and the offices extended in 1824 are crowned with Dutch gables like overgrown dolls' houses.

The controversial approach and forecourt were the work of the landscape architect, William Nesfield. He was embellishing a Jacobean house built in 1616 by a junior branch of the Wilbraham family. It was sold in 1754, and the ground floor was much altered by William Baker in the 1750s and later by Samuel Wyatt. The house passed through Tollemaches (including the aggrieved wife) to the present descendants, the Roundells, who are now restoring each room in turn.

The interior reflects the familiar tension of Jacobean original and later modernization. The hall gives onto the dining room by Baker, containing some fine Morland landscapes. To the rear is a light, sunny library with a ceiling in the Adam style. The plasterwork depicts rustic themes and contains two billing and cooing doves, said to represent a wedding.

Upstairs, Jacobean survives. A staircase with flat balusters leads to the house's centrepiece, the Great Chamber above the old hall. Its barrel-vaulted plaster ceiling, created in 1621, is one of the most intricate anywhere. The craftsmen are thought to be the same as worked in the Great Chamber at Lyme. Emblems of rose, thistle and fleur-de-lys celebrate the union of England, Scotland and (English) France. The strapwork, extended to the end walls and frieze, is of phenomenal complexity. There are Tudor pendants, as if the still-wet plaster had begun to drip and form stalactites. On the walls are 17th-century and later portraits, including bold ones of present-day Roundells by Howard Morgan.

From the windows can be seen the fields over which generations of owners indulged the Cheshire passion for hunting.

Right Six new bathrooms were created at Dunham Massey when the house was renovated by the 9th Earl. The Stamford bathroom retains its original Edwardian fittings, including the 10th Earl's crocodile-skin travel toilet case.

Dunham Massey

★★★ Georgian house with Edwardian restoration

At Dunham Town, 8 miles E of Warrington; National Trust, open part year

For almost two centuries Dunham Massey has clung to life, neglected by its owners and besieged by Greater Manchester. Yet it survives, protected by its park and estate. Its rooms are restored and a branch of the family who built it, the Stamfords, remain as National Trust tenants. Their standard flies from the flagpole when they are in residence (lowered only during the Falklands War because it is nearly identical to the Argentine flag).

The present house owes its existence to George Booth, 2nd Earl of Warrington. He inherited the Dunham estate at the age of nineteen in 1694, traumatized by seeing his reckless father 'aweeping for the greatness of his debts' and dying at forty-two. Booth married the daughter of a London merchant purely for her £40,000 dowry. He paid off his father's debts, rebuilt the house, produced a daughter and lived apart from his wife, his duty done. The daughter married Harry Grey, 4th Earl of Stamford. The house prospered until the gambling 7th Earl married a circus rider and was so disliked locally that they left Dunham for good.

The title and property eventually settled on a dissolute clergyman married to a Hottentot in South Africa. His possibly illegitimate son, John, claimed the Dunham estate and had to be bought off by the trustees. Great Britain was deprived of surely its only Hottentot aristocrat, who went to live in Worthing. In 1906, a Canadian clergyman arrived as 9th Earl, a liberal and enthusiastic archaeologist, only to die three years later. His son was so dominated by his mother that he refused to marry. He occupied just three rooms next to his mother's and became an active peer and model landlord. He supported the United Nations and entertained Haile Selassie, passing the property in good order to the National Trust on his death in 1976.

Family history is the most exciting thing about Dunham. The house, which the 2nd Earl of Warrington refashioned in the 1730s, is grand, beautifully displayed and a little dull. The exterior is a

large redbrick box with plain stone centrepiece, enlivened only by an Edwardian alteration to the roof. The east and north fronts are plain, the former graced with a semi-circular bow on top of which the 10th Earl laid out a garden for Haile Selassie during his stay.

The entrance hall is in the south front. Until the 20th century, this was a dark passage to the courtyard, the entrance leading, medieval style, into the Great Hall on its far side. To the right of the present hall is the 20th-century Lady Stamford's suite and to the left the rooms of her son, the 10th and last Earl. Her parlour has been retained as she left it in 1959, embodying the neatness of genteel poverty that 'reuses envelopes and saves string'.

The saloon, a Georgian replacement for the old Great Parlour, is furnished as an Edwardian drawing room. The Stamford portraits are mostly by Romney. The room contains lovely satinwood bookcases, a touch of Georgian levity amid the Edwardian solemnity. Beyond is the Great Hall; the present room is grand, with yellow walls and plasterwork in the style of Inigo Jones. What might be a cold room was turned by the Edwardian 9th Earl into a furnished and carpeted drawing room. Behind the Great Hall is

a surprise, a small chapel, simple and severe as befitted the staunchly Protestant Booths. It is beautifully panelled, with 'Wren' pilasters on either side of the altar.

During the Great War, hospital operations were performed on the landing at the top of the Grand Staircase. The Earl's sister, Lady Jane Turnbull, held a torch for the surgeons. The Great Gallery beyond is hung with five paintings of the Dunham estate in the 1690s and again in the 1750s, the most remarkable topographical survey of any country house and its grounds to remain *in situ*. The long avenues are still in place, but nature has been allowed to destroy their precision and drama. In the same gallery is the Dunham Guercino, an *Allegory of Time*, and a magnificent portrait of Lord Warrington's mastiff, *Old Vertue*.

The lovely library, filled with leather-bound volumes, has over its fireplace Grinling Gibbons' early masterpiece, *The Crucifixion*. This was based on Tintoretto's similar work in the Scuola di San Rocco in Venice. Below is the 10th Earl's study, left full of the paperwork and clutter of a busy man of affairs. Outside rests his bicycle. The excellent service rooms are all restored and include 'one of the largest Agas ever made'.

Gawsworth hall

★★☆ Black-and-white Tudor manor house

At Gawsworth, 3 miles SW of Macclesfield; private house, open part year

Those despairing the fate of the English country house need look no further than Gawsworth. Since the Richards family acquired it in 1962, a family home has blossomed into weddings, concerts, live theatre and opera. Talk here about the 'Glyndebourne of the North' and you receive a sniffy retort about the 'Gawsworth of the South'. Who needs National Trusts and Heritage Lotteries when there are Richardses about? But then there is money in Cheshire.

Like most black-and-white houses, Gawsworth is heavily restored. The first owners were the Fitton family, knights in the Wars of the Roses and ancestors of Mary Fitton, briefly maid of honour

Above The ambulatory at Gawsworth Hall contains a font and also serves as a family baptistry. Among the stained-glass windows that light its walls are four made by William Morris to designs by Edward Burne-Jones. These depict Saints Agnes, George, Stephen and Alban.

to Elizabeth I and mistress of the Earl of Pembroke. She was a dedicatee of Shakespeare's First Folio and a candidate for the 'dark lady'. Her father laid out gardens and built a tilting ground in the hope of a Royal visit that never came. The house was bought by the Stanhope family and tenanted for much of its life. Fittons still return from across the world for reunions.

Gawsworth's main front is much restored, but the three-sided courtyard behind is a black-and-white delight. The three-storey jettied bay on the far wing has original window leading. The interiors are warm and cluttered. The library contains bookcases by A. W. N. Pugin (from Scarisbrick) and Timothy Richards's car racing goggles (he is a Morgan enthusiast). Above the staircase hangs a Waterford crystal chandelier, apparently found in a wheelbarrow. A small chapel appears to date from 1701 but recalls chapels on this site since 1365. The Richards family has built a small ambulatory to hold a set of William Morris windows which, with other furnishings, came from a redundant church in Ipswich.

An original Great Hall, now truncated, may survive as the Green Drawing Room. Upstairs are more variations on a Tudor theme, including priest's holes dating from the late 16th century. Each bedroom seems more voluptuous than the last, with beams darting out of walls and overhangs looming above ancient panelling. More shocking is a 1950s vitriolite bathroom, apparently listed for preservation.

An RSJ has been inserted in the library ceiling to support a billiard table above. Here the Richards's eccentricity reaches new heights. In among billiard cues and family portraits are a reclining statue of the goddess Echo and a huge devotional altarpiece. The gardens at Gawsworth embrace the remains of the tilting ground. Excavations of what may be extensive Tudor pleasure grounds are in hand.

Highfields

★ Elizabethan manor with Victorian renovations

At Audlem, 5 miles S of Nantwich; private house, open for tours by arrangement

Highfields is a black-and-white yeoman's manor of which Cheshire must once have boasted hundreds. The house sits alone across the fields at a distance from its farm. The land was owned by the Dod family, apparently since Saxon times, and they built the present house, completing it in 1615. It passed by marriage to the architect, William Baker, in 1736 and is owned by Bakers to this day.

The exterior is remarkable for its symmetry and the generosity of its side wings, each of one bay but 13 timbers width. The porch is centred and decorated with pretty Gothic panels. The Victorians added aggressive neo-Tudor chimneys and a large drawing room at the back. They stuccoed the exterior but this has since been removed.

The interior saw the importation in the 19th century of much panelling and fireplaces, posing an impossible problem to those seeking to know what is original, imported or Victorian reproduction. It is of no consequence. Highfields is a cosy nest of vernacular carvings, portraits and horse paintings. Its passages seem redolent of dogs and huntsmen. Time and period do not matter.

All the downstairs rooms have fine fireplaces, the best in the Oak Room having cartouches and Corinthian orders. The hall fireplace is decorated with musicians. The drawing room is hung with family Knellers and Hudsons. Dods and Bakers might have been modest gentry but they visited London, sent their sons to Oxford and commissioned the best portraits. The staircase has two-strand barley sugar balusters and an old alms chest for bread for the poor. During my visit, a hunt at full canter thundered past outside.

Little Moreton hall

★★☆ Medieval and Tudor manor house, built around a courtyard

4 miles SW of Congleton; National Trust, open part year

What are we to make of this place? At first sight Little Moreton is fresh from Disneyland. Neat, clean and tumbledown, it looks ready for a princess to appear from a casement, a ghost to clank from the gatehouse and a monster to rise from the moat. It seems to taunt the laws of gravity, like a pack of cards which might at any moment collapse.

Yet Little Moreton is as real as the National Trust restorers will allow. The house plan is familiar. A gatehouse gives onto an internal courtyard with the Great Hall beyond, built by Sir Richard de Moreton in about 1450. Service wings are to the left and solar and chapel to the right.

The guest chambers on the first floor of the gatehouse came later, along with lavish bay windows (1559) in the Great Hall and Old Parlour. Finally, in the 1580s, a Long Gallery was added across the top of the gatehouse wing. This is an astonishing structure, above a range that seems ill-suited to support it.

The most remarkable thing about this house is its survival. The Moretons were local magnates, challenging the Wilbrahams of Rode to 'sit first in church'. They suffered for taking the Royalist side in the Civil War and abandoned the house to tenant farmers. With the rise of the Picturesque movement in the 19th century, the house became celebrated. The watercolourist, John Sell Cotman, visited it in 1806 and found chickens in the Great Hall. Yet Moretons continued to take an interest in the house. It was inherited by a nun, Elizabeth Moreton, who was devoted to its preservation. She passed it to a cousin by marriage, Bishop Abraham of Derby, who ensured its orderly transfer to the National Trust in 1938.

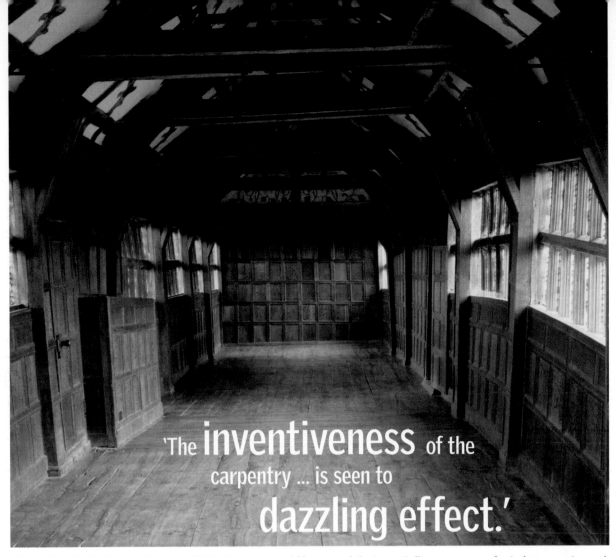

'The **inventiveness** of the carpentry ... is seen to **dazzling effect.**'

Above The Elizabethan inhabitants of Little Moreton would have used the Long Gallery as a space for indoor exercise and playing games – several long-lost, early 17th-century tennis balls have been found behind the panelling – and therefore the room would have contained only a few pieces of furniture.

Apart from its sheer quaintness, the house is chiefly of archaeological interest, a place for students of beams, trusses, braces, crown-posts and purlins. It has oversailing and coving galore. The studding is open, diagonal and quatrefoil. The inventiveness of the carpentry in a county devoid of brick and stone is seen to dazzling effect. Little Moreton was being completed by William Moreton when Hardwick (see page 79) and Wollaton, in Nottinghamshire, were already under construction. It was an old-fashioned house, except in its extravagant use of glass. The motifs carved into its lintels and bargeboards seem exclusively medieval.

The parlour has fragments of painted panelling, the withdrawing room a fine octagonal table. The chapel is curious, a tiny nave with a chancel that rises two storeys, facing a 'prayer room' above. Most spectacular is the Long Gallery. It is panelled but with extensive fenestration and heavy roof members to support a stone-tiled roof. At each end are primitive plaster reliefs, depicting Destiny and the Wheel of Fortune. A woman is dressed like a Botticelli angel.

The National Trust has left the interior empty. The rooms have little to distinguish them and few merit description. The guide explains that the interior has been empty for most of the past three centuries, offering an opportunity to 'appreciate its structural ingenuity'. That is fine for archaeologists, but little fun for the rest of us. In the 1940s, the then-resident custodian, Mrs Dale, dispensed scrambled eggs with scones and tea while hens scrabbled in the courtyard and cows approached from the meadow. We could do with more of that today.

Lyme park

★★★★ Aristocratic Elizabethan mansion, transformed by Leoni

6½ miles SE of Stockport; National Trust, open part year

The noblest house in the north-west is still darkened by the tale of Lord Newton's surrender to the National Trust in 1946. James Lees-Milne wrote: 'The world is too much for him, and no wonder. He does not know what he can do, ought to do or wants to do. He just throws up his hands in despair. The only thing he is sure about is that his descendants will never live at Lyme after an unbroken residence of 600 years.' The heartbreak was shared with a hundred owners at that time.

The family had acquired Lyme by force of arms, an ancestor being awarded a Cheshire hunting lodge for saving the Black Prince at Crècy. It was Sir Piers Legh who built the Elizabethan house and succeeding generations who added to it and altered it. Giacomo Leoni transformed the exterior and much of the interior after 1725. Here, on the flanks of the Pennines, he converted an old courtyard house into a monument to the Grand Tour. The grandest in the land danced and laughed through its halls and saloons. The park was studded with classical follies. The estate boasted its own breed of cattle and its own breed of mastiff.

'The **grandest** in the land **danced ...**
through its halls and saloons.'

Above After passing under the Elizabethan frontispiece of the North Front (below left), the visitor to Lyme steps into the Palladian courtyard, fashioned in the style of an Italian *palazzo*. Leoni set a massive Doric doorway at the eastern end, approached by a double flight of stone stairs.

Lyme then languished. It was revived by a dashing Thomas Legh in the 19th century and saw a final glow under Newton descendants in the years before the Great War. The subsequent horrors of taxation and loss of staff demoralized the family and led to the house's abrupt surrender. All was gone. Lord Newton's sister wrote that the windows were 'as blind eyes or eyes closed in sleep'.

The house today is a fine relic of Cheshire aristocracy. A sweeping drive drops down from the main road along a deep ravine. The park was a medieval deer park, enclosed *c*1400 but never extensively landscaped. The massive house appears round a bend in the valley as a *coup de théâtre*, brilliantly exploited as Darcy's mansion in the television serialisation of 'Pride and Prejudice'.

The welcoming façade is odd, composed of an earlier range with Elizabethan frontispiece of 1570. Four tiers of classical orders support a statue of Minerva. The other façades are Palladian, the orders Ionic, the stone cold and grey. The internal courtyard, however, is a total contrast, an essay in the Italian Renaissance. Rusticated colonnades support a *piano nobile*, entered by double flights of steps into a majestic doorway.

From outside, we expect Lyme's interiors to be monotonously classical. Yet enough rooms survive from the Elizabethan house to ensure that the rooms are never dull. Leoni's entrance hall is a sort of overblown drawing room, with an Edwardian Baroque overmantel and copious gilding. A frame reveals a Georgian portrait

of the family's benefactor, the Black Prince, which swings out from the old Great Chamber above, thus enabling the chamber to become a gallery. The hall is hung with Mortlake tapestries. The carpet is said to be designed by A. W. N. Pugin.

Steps lead from the hall to the Great Chamber, now called the drawing room. This could not be a greater contrast from the hall. It is a room of Jacobean richness and romance. The ceiling is of delicate strapwork. Above the Renaissance fireplace is the coat of arms of Elizabeth I. Stained glass, some of it medieval, adds to the air of mystery. Beyond lies the Stag Parlour, decorated on the theme of the life of a stag. Here was plotted, and aborted, the Cheshire conspiracy in favour of the Jacobite rebellion. This dangerous moment is thought to be the origin of the Lyme tradition of men retiring from the dining room for port rather than remaining at table when the ladies have left.

The dining room was reconstructed by Lewis Wyatt in the 19th century, yet based on its 17th-century decoration, including the Gibbons-style carving for walls and fireplace. From here at breakfast Lord Newton would look out to see if the Lantern Tower on the hillside was visible. If it was, he knew he could go shooting.

Leoni's saloon is on the south front, the start of the state room sequence. The wood panelling and florid Rococo ceiling are probably original to Leoni, but it was Wyatt who inserted the Grinling Gibbons carvings from the present dining room. They are the glory of the room. Wyatt shows his

Above left When Lewis Wyatt remodelled the saloon at Lyme he placed a large plate-glass mirror opposite the entrance to the room. Mounted in a frame resembling a doorway, the mirror created the illusion of a continuing enfilade to anyone who looked into the saloon from the library opposite. **Above right** Wyatt returned the drawing room, once the Great Chamber, to its Jacobean splendour. The stained glass was inserted at this time and includes pieces taken from medieval churches and armorial panes dating from the 16th and 17th centuries.

respect for Gibbons by placing each composition in the centre of a panel in place of a picture, celebrating the craftsman as artist.

The staircase has been redecorated in a Victorian dark red. This is perhaps in honour of the giant moose's head that dominates the space. Upstairs is the Elizabethan Long Gallery, used by the Edwardian family for theatricals and for distributing gifts to estate staff. Two sofas are available for exhausted visitors. The ceiling is Jacobean reproduction and the pictures of worthies come from the National Portrait Gallery.

Of the bedrooms the most impressive is the Knight's Room, with a bulbous four-poster, stylish overmantel and a bold strapwork ceiling. A secret passage is said to lead from here to the Cage Tower on the hill. It was here that the 2nd Lord Newton's mother-in-law took to sleeping, convinced that the house was overrun with burglars. The gardens at Lyme are a blessed lung on the edge of the Peak District, the closest open space to the Manchester conurbation.

Peckforton castle

⭐ ⭐ Victorian castle by Salvin, high on a crag

11½ miles SE of Chester; now a hotel

Peckforton crowns a rocky outcrop in the Cheshire plain. Its towers burst through a thick skirt of forest to glower across at Beeston on a neighbouring outcrop. They are like two giants preparing for combat. Whereas Beeston's towers are medieval, Peckforton's were built afresh by Anthony Salvin for Lord Tollemache in 1844.

The location reminds me of the castle of Sintra outside Lisbon. A winding track leads up through dripping woods to reach a huge gatehouse set in red stone walls. From this vantage point his lordship could command his 26,000 acres of Cheshire with the splendour of a feudal lord. Tollemache was, according to Mark Girouard, 'one of those tremendous rock-hewn Victorians who seem built on a larger scale than ordinary men'. He had twelve children and was a model landowner who rehoused all his tenants in the surrounding villages. Gladstone much admired him.

The most remarkable feature of the castle is its site. It is as if Windsor had fled north on a stormy night. The tower with its battlemented walls and lesser towers stands out from the trees as sentinels. The gatehouse gives onto a wide courtyard with the Great Hall opposite and the domestic and services ranges on either side. A large tree has been left in the middle for picturesque effect.

The interiors are of cold Gothic stone, invigorating, precise and scholarly. The drama of the staircase is exceeded only by Lutyens at Castle Drogo in Devon, of which this is reminiscent.

The main rooms have rib-vaulted roofs and stone-mullioned windows. Yet their uses were those of a typical Victorian villa – dining room, drawing room, gallery and, next to the gatehouse, a small chapel.

Peover hall

⭐⭐⭐ Elizabethan manor house with remarkable stables

At Over Peover, 9 miles W of Macclesfield; private house, open part year

The old seat of the Cheshire Mainwarings was built in 1585 and acquired by a Mancunian furniture tycoon, Harry Brooks, in 1940. Today, Peover Hall describes itself as a 'working' house. This means that the Brookses respect its history but are content to alter it to suit their needs. Wings have been demolished, rooms reordered, contemporary fittings inserted from elsewhere. Books, papers, discarded clothes and unmade beds are a feature of any visit. The place feels lived in with a vengeance.

The oddity of the house is immediately apparent outside. A range of gabled rooms is attached to a neo-Elizabethan brick façade, like a converted keep. This façade was built in the 1960s after the demolition of a Georgian wing. The resulting interior has no formal plan and is an enjoyable jumble of insertions that makes little sense and does not matter. We wander through a maze of old rooms, corridors and attics.

This is a house that draws on many houses. The Great Hall is made from old kitchens, with two large fireplaces facing each other. The walls, painted a jolly yellow, are hung with Mainwaring arms and armour. There are two magnificent dressers, one decorated with Knights of the Round Table, the other with scenes from *Pilgrim's Progress*.

The parlour and dining room have been restored with panelling from other Mainwaring properties. The parlour's overmantel has a frieze of scenes from the life of Julius Caesar and a sedan chair displaying porcelain. In the dining room, the Corinthian pilasters have been 'silver-leafed' with chocolate silver paper by members of the family over the years. It is a delightful touch that would give the National Trust apoplexy and never be permitted in any of their properties.

A Georgian staircase rises to a landing of charming pomposity, with lofty ceilings and ornate cornices, hung with portraits of Hanoverian monarchs. They include a superb George III by Lawrence. This forms an ante-room to the drawing room, with panelling and bookcases from a Mainwaring house at Oteley in Shropshire. Here hangs a copy of van Dyck's celebrated portrait of the Jacobean statesman, Thomas Wentworth, Earl of Strafford, with his secretary, a Mainwaring.

Peover has a splendid set of old bedrooms. One has a Flemish bed with unusual sliding door panels. This room offers a view over the finest feature of Peover's garden, an array of yew hedges and free-standing yew obelisks. A complex yew pattern has also been created round the swimming pool, a modernist's re-creation of a medieval knot garden. The attic is a Long Gallery, with scissorbeams overhead and family junk in every alcove. Here are toy engines and yachts, chairs, pictures, rocking horses and children's books galore.

The stables at Peover are more highly 'listed' than the house. They were built in 1654 and are of a type once common but now of the greatest rarity. By coincidence, similar stables remain at another Mainwaring house, Whitmore Hall (see page 180).

The horses are accorded classical stalls which have arches and a strapwork frieze. The ceiling is worthy of a Restoration drawing room. Sadly, there are no horses in residence.

The ceiling is **worthy** of a **Restoration** **drawing room.'**

Quarry Bank Mill:
The Apprentice house

⭐ Basic housing for child millworkers

At Styal, 7 miles NW of Macclesfield; National Trust, open part year

Quarry Bank Mill lurks in a deep ravine in the wooded valley of the River Bollin. The spot was selected in 1783 by Samuel Greg for his water-powered spinning machine. It became one of the largest mills in the country. Here, a century and a half later in 1939, his great-great-grandson Alec imaginatively donated the still-working mill with its estate and village of Styal to the National Trust. The mill was in production until 1959. It is now fully restored, partly working and open to the public.

Above the mill buildings is the house where the apprentices lived. Such was the shortage of labour that young people were brought from workhouses and orphanages to be 'trained', which in reality meant they worked unpaid in the mill for up to seven years. Almost a third of the mill workers in the early years were children, some as young as seven. Greg was regarded as a benevolent employer but the system was hard, only a step better than the workhouse. Children received food and clothing and the rudiments of reading, writing and counting.

The Quarry Bank house could take up to 100 apprentices and was overcrowded. Visible today is the schoolroom, complete with slates, candles and admonitions to hard work. Next door is the kitchen where porridge (and little else but occasional broth) was prepared and eaten. Outside is a small garden where the children could grow vegetables to supplement their diet. Upstairs are two dormitories for girls and boys. Greg preferred the former as girls were 'less truculent' and needed less sleeping space. They slept two to a box bed on a straw mattress, replaced once a year.

The chief hazard to Quarry Bank today is the NT tour, timed and conducted with Victorian strictness. It is aimed at primary school children and is no place for grown-ups of any age.

Right The Apprentice House had a sick room where mild illnesses could be treated with simple home remedies, often made from herbs grown in the garden. Serious cases might be attended by Dr Holland, the Knutsford doctor responsible for the children's health.

Rode hall

★★ Eighteenth-century house with portrait and porcelain collections

5 miles SW of Congleton; private house, open by arrangement

When a woman marries a man she customarily takes his name. Not so among the English landed classes. It depends who had the bigger estate. When a Miss Wilbraham of Rode married a Mr Baker in 1872, it was he who changed his name. There had been Wilbrahams at Rode for more than three centuries and the lack of a male heir was neither here nor there. The house is a Wilbraham home and they 'will continue to live here for many years to come' says the present owner, Sir Richard Wilbraham.

The pleasing redbrick house looks from the drive like two houses semi-detached, one Queen Anne the other mid-Georgian. That to the right of the main door has two storeys with a cupola and Venetian windows. That to the left is of 1752, later amended with a pillared loggia in front of the entrance.

The house is chiefly of interest for the present Sir Richard's collection of china and porcelain, attracting a constant stream of admirers. Almost as impressive is the continuous line of family portraits, from Joshua Reynolds

through Walter Crane to the present day. The modern works are a relief from the usual staid historical depictions.

Beyond the pillared entrance hall is a generous staircase, surviving from the 18th century, with wide treads and Rococo plasterwork. Much of the furniture is by Gillow of Lancaster, notably the superb bookcases in the library. Many of the books were those of the medical collection of the Baker family, Sir George Baker being one of the doctors attending George III in his madness. Sir George is pictured in the drawing room.

The best formal room is the dining room, designed by Lewis Wyatt in a severely classical style and with a Gillow sideboard of 1813 in an apsidal alcove. With its scagliola columns and walls in shades of green, the room on a sunny day can seem to be floating underwater.

Humphry Repton contributed a Red Book for Rode but we do not know to what effect. William Nesfield was later involved in the formal gardens. The grounds have been superbly restored by the present Wilbrahams.

Tabley house

Palladian mansion by Carr of York

4 miles NE of Northwich; private house, open part year

Tabley boasts itself the 'finest Palladian mansion in the North-West'. The house from the lake, with its well-formed portico and curving double staircase, is a splendid sight. The clutter of entrance, stables and service buildings round the courtyard are relegated to the rear.

Tabley was owned by the Leicester family for seven centuries. The former old hall was on an island in the lake. The new house was designed by Carr of York in 1761 and remained in the family until the last of the line died unmarried in 1975. The house was refused by the National Trust for lacking endowment and passed to the Victoria University of Manchester. It was then leased to a health care company as a nursing home, the main rooms being handed to a trust. The arrangement seems to work.

Access to the main reception rooms is from the south front, Carr's original entrance, up his magnificent sweep of steps. The rooms are chiefly of interest for the surviving paintings of the Leicester collection. Most were dispersed in a sale in 1827, after being refused by the government as the basis for a National Gallery.

The drawing room offers a Dobson of the 1st Lord Byron in the Civil War and Turner's depiction of Tabley from a distance across the lake 'on a windy day'. It also displays the dramatic *Destruction of Herculaneum and Pompeii* by John Martin, Queen Victoria's favourite historical artist.

In the Common Parlour next door is the old manorial rent table and a set of Devis pictures of the house from different angles. The parlour contains a rare 'anamorphic' picture of either Charles I or Charles II, designed for Jacobites to worship covertly on the inside of a cylinder.

The main picture gallery was created early in the 19th century from three rooms along the west front, now divided only by shallow classical arches. The furniture includes Chippendale mirrors, console tables and sofas by Gillow of Lancaster. The paintings are ghosts of the great Leicester collection, with works by Fuseli, Lawrence and Northcote. Houses with public exhibitions such as Tabley should surely be given a choice of finer works now languishing in the basements of London galleries.

Tatton old hall

⭐ Brick-clad medieval hall house

At Tatton, 7 miles NE of Northwich; museum, open part year for tours

The great house of the Egerton family is unusual in retaining, half a mile across its park, the old hall which it supplanted. Hidden behind a clump of trees, alive with rooks, stands the Old Hall, like an embarrassing great-aunt who refuses to die. While crowds pack the main house, the Old Hall is neglected, possibly because of its hour-long tour.

The medieval hall was built *c*1520 for the Brereton family and acquired by the Egertons in 1598. It was soon leased to tenants and later divided into three farmers' cottages, the black-and-white walls encased in brick. The Great Hall is excellently displayed, with a central fire, tapestry and high table, although the display of 'medieval' catering seems earlier than the Tudor architecture. The place reeks satisfactorily of wood smoke.

The rest of the building has been restored more or less to its 19th-century form. The rear quarters are variously 17th, 19th and 20th century. Upstairs from the Hall is a bedroom of the early 17th century with hangings of the period and furniture from the original inventory. The remaining rooms are arranged as a museum, and are well done.

Tatton park

★★☆ Grand Palladian mansion by the Wyatt dynasty

At Tatton, 7 miles NE of Northwich; National Trust, open part year

Tatton is the grandest of the great Cheshire houses. When it was given to the National Trust by the 4th Baron Egerton in 1958, its rooms, furniture and art were intact. Only the 25,000 acres of Tatton land that had once rolled uninterrupted to the Derbyshire hills had gone. What remains is 2,000 acres, laid out by Repton, with avenues of limes and a deer park, a precious lung for the people of Manchester.

Tatton was first built in 1716 but rebuilt slowly after 1780 in a neo-classical style, by Samuel Wyatt and his nephew, Lewis. The house from the outside looks formal and almost modest, its garden front that of a grey Palladian villa two storeys high with portico and hipped roof. Yet this is a giant house, its rear quarters well concealed. The basement is so extensive as to have a small railway to carry coal from the back door to the main house.

'... this is a **giant house,** its rear quarters **well concealed.'**

Left In the basement at Tatton Park, in the 'below-stairs' world of service areas and servants, there is a passage that runs the length of the building. Set into its floor is a trolley 'railway', complete with turntable, that allowed servants to transport heavy or awkward loads, such as coal or luggage, beneath the house. That such a labour-saving device was necessary gives some idea of how much work was involved in running a house of Tatton's size.

The interior is mostly a gallery of pictures and Egerton furniture, the latter notably by Gillow. The entrance hall shows the Wyatts at their most Graeco-Roman, with porphyry columns and coved ceiling with classical motifs. On the wall is a painting by Henry Calvert of the Cheshire Hunt, with Egertons in the van. Here too is an exquisite Portuguese jewel cabinet from Goa, inlaid with tortoiseshell and green-stained ivory.

Four reception rooms sit round the staircase hall. The walls of the music room are hung in cherry-red silk damask. The alcove bookshelves contain leather-bound scores. Opposite hangs Guercino's *Absalom and Tamar*.

The library is the most casual of the state rooms. It contains one of the National Trust's largest collections, 8,000 volumes in this room alone. Here are globes, book presses, movable stairs, chairs for reading books of differing sizes, card tables, chess tables and writing implements galore. It is a chamber inviting scholarship, a marvellous room. Through the windows on a clear day can be seen Bosley Cloud on the Cheshire–Derbyshire border 13 miles away, once Egerton land too.

The rest of the house marks a change of key. The wide formal staircase, lit by Lewis Wyatt's lovely domes and receding arches, is crowned by ten portraits of The Cheshire Gentlemen. This is the conspiracy that gathered (at Lyme Park) to discuss whether to support the Jacobite rising of 1715, wisely deciding against.

The 'below stairs' quarters at Tatton are among the most comprehensive in any great house. They are displayed with National Trust thoroughness, with not a speck of dust and every brass pot gleaming.

Winnington hall

★ Georgian house by Samuel Wyatt

At Winnington, 1 mile NW of Northwich; private house, open by arrangement

This is for addicts. Next to the Trent and Mersey Canal and between a derelict chemical works and an ICI treatment plant is the house bought in 1872 from Lord Stanley by two immigrant engineers, Ludwig Mond and John Brunner. Here began the future ICI. The house is now a club and venue for hire. The house would once have looked out on a wooded hillside across the fields north of Northwich.

Today the setting is undeniably sad. The mansion is of *c*1780 and immensely stylish, in hard blackened stone with a spattering of Adam motifs on the front and side elevations. It is by Samuel Wyatt of the architectural clan ubiquitous at this time in Cheshire. To the rear is a substantial black-and-white building, a victorianized 17th-century work now housing a series of bars. Brunner had this part while Mond took the Wyatt side. There is no doubt who had the better deal.

The Wyatt interiors are excellent. A gallery forms a corridor behind the main reception rooms, with a coved ceiling, attached columns, fans in panels and Greek medallions. It might be a miniature Tatton.

Derby

shire

Chatsworth

Derbyshire

Barlborough hall

★ ★ Elizabethan mansion attributed to Robert Smythson

Near Barlborough, 7 miles W of Worksop; private house, open by arrangement

From a distance, Barlborough is a miniature Hardwick. Lofty towers of honeyed Derbyshire stone rise above a feast of windows. This is no rough Tudor hall. It displays the compact Renaissance symmetry of Robert Smythson. A stone's throw from the M1, Barlborough is a jewel in its landscape.

The house was built by an Elizabethan judge, Sir Francis Rodes, whose patron was Bess of Hardwick's husband, the Earl of Shrewsbury. He was thus in the Smythson orbit. The date on the outside is 1583.

The house remained in the Rodes family, later named Locker-Lampson, until the 1930s when the house was sold to the Jesuits for a prep. school which it remains today. Every stick of furniture and any removable fittings were sold, a truly tragic loss from a house of such importance. Conversion into a school has spoiled most of the interior with partitions and cheap furniture. The rooms are shown on request but the exterior of Barlborough is best. The house sits on a high basement, with internal chimneys and corner towers, all Smythson signatures. The whole building seems to be straining after verticality. This is a wonderfully poised composition, English architecture at the moment of its emergence from the dark Middle Ages into the light of Reason.

Inside, the reception rooms are arranged round a narrow internal courtyard, now glazed. Of surviving fragments, the Great Chamber is used as a chapel and retains a 1584 overmantel. This is formal and classical, carrying the coats of arms of Rodes and his two wives. The contrast could hardly be greater with the adjacent parlour. Its overmantel of 1697 is alive with New World motifs and acanthus leaves.

Other rooms are smothered in ubiquitous school notices, pasted watercolours and other paraphernalia. In one, I glimpsed a delightful dolphin frieze.

Bolsover castle

✦✦✦✧ Renaissance palace built in the form of a fantasy castle

At Bolsover, 6 miles E of Chesterfield; English Heritage, open all year

First, forget the idea of castle. Seen from the M1, Bolsover may look like a fortress but it is rather a fairytale palace on a hill. Bolsover was built on the basis of an earlier keep by Sir Charles Cavendish, son of Bess of Hardwick, whose own house stands on the same ridge four miles to the south. Working with John Smythson (son of Robert) from 1612, Cavendish intended Bolsover's Little Castle to be the embodiment of Elizabethan Renaissance romanticism and refinement continued into the reign of James I. It was a folly, a morality tale, a Shakespearean conceit, architecture as lovers' masque.

Charles Cavendish died in 1616 before the project was complete and building was resumed by his son, William. The latter entered fully into the spirit of his father's imagination, now asking Smythson for an additional palace adjacent to the Little Castle. To this, he added a Riding House round an inner courtyard. These additions, now mostly ruined, are hugely exciting works of Stuart architecture.

... the embodiment of Elizabethan Renaissance romanticism ...'

There are thus two separate elements to Renaissance Bolsover, the one still Elizabethan in ethos, the other Jacobean and ostentatious. To understand these two elements, one must understand William Cavendish, a man of his new age. In total contrast to his domineering, essentially medieval, grandmother, Bess of Hardwick, he displayed courtly life at its most engaging and fastidious. 'Ceremony,' he wrote, 'though it is nothing in itself, yet it does everything.' He travelled like a French courtier, his equestrian retinue trained to perfection. At soldiering, Cavendish was useless. When called on to defend the North for the King in the Civil War, he failed at Marston Moor in 1644 and fled to the Continent. For this and for his preference for 'sweet company' he was not forgiven by many Royalists, yet at the Restoration he was made Duke of Newcastle and allowed to complete his palace.

His descendants eventually moved the contents of Bolsover to their seat at Welbeck and the old castle and palace became derelict. The outer walls still stand and the Riding House, with shoeing hall and stable building, remains complete and is even used for riding lessons. The Little Castle beyond became a rectory in the 19th century before passing to the government in 1945. It has been superbly restored by English Heritage.

The walk through the Great Court displays these contrasting styles and uses. To the left, the spreading walls of William's palace reveal superb views over the valley below. The outside aspect of these walls is unlike anything in England: giant rusticated pilasters and pedimented windows form a façade of Baroque robustness.

Above left The decoration of the fireplace in the Star Chamber includes statues of two talbots, the hunting dogs of the Shrewsbury family, owners of a former keep on the site of Bolsover Castle. Paintings of prophets and saints line the walls.
Above right The paintings in the Pillar Parlour depict the Five Senses, while the bosses on the vaulted ceiling are in the shape of horses heads, possibly reflecting Sir William's equestrian interests.

The Little Castle beyond is reached through a wall to the Fountain Garden. Here a lawn, once presumably a knot garden, is overlooked by a Renaissance 'Romeo and Juliet' window. The interiors, begun by Charles and completed by William, are unequalled in England as expressions of Elizabethan romanticism. The Little Castle was built, wrote Mark Girouard, 'not for genuine barons of the Middle Ages ... but for the half-allegorical knights and ladies of Spenser, Sidney and Ariosto, with names like Florimel, Calepine and Triamond'. The cult of the Virgin Queen gave rise to an obsession with medieval chivalry and fantastical contests of courtly love. Ceremonial tournaments were held in the yard below, albeit with few injuries.

The stone chambers of the Little Castle are part medieval, part Serlian Renaissance in style. The decorative themes are those of the literary and emotional obsession of late-Elizabethan England. To the left of the entrance is an ante-room with wall-paintings depicting the humours, melancholic, choleric and phlegmatic. The fourth, sanguinity, was represented by William himself. Next door is the hall, with a vaulted ceiling, mock Gothic fireplace and murals of the Labours of Hercules. Here

William and his friends dressed in medieval costume and prepared for jousts and lovers' trysts.

The adjacent Pillar Parlour is nothing short of sensational, possibly copied by Smythson from the Great Parlour in the vanished Cecil palace of Theobalds in Hertfordshire. It has murals of the Senses and richly embossed panelling beneath classicized Gothic vaulting. It may have been here that Charles I and his Queen received their 'stupendous entertainment' in 1634. The feast reputedly cost Cavendish £15,000 and left him debt-ridden for life.

The parlour is rivalled only by the Star Chamber upstairs. The ceiling has geometrical panels painted blue and with stars. The wall-paintings represent Old Testament figures. Two smaller rooms depict Heaven and Elysium, both with ceilings of cherubs and musicians, cupids and gods. Heaven is said to be painted in shell gold, '400 times more expensive even than gold leaf'. The ceiling of Elysium, home of the gods, is copied from the palace at Fontainebleau. It was so well crafted as never to have needed substantive restoration.

In each of these rooms is a fireplace, Gothic or classical in style, idiosyncratic and symbolic of the surrounding theme. The fireplaces of Bolsover are a book in themselves. The windows look down on the garden and the Venus Fountain with its 23 statues. It carries the inscription 'All is but vanite', a sardonic postscript on the Castle of Love.

Calke abbey

★★★ Country house cluttered with the relics of centuries

At Calke, 10 miles S of Derby; National Trust, open part year

The picture on the cover of the guidebook says it all. Stag-head trophies lie upturned on an old bed and in an open grate. Round them are scattered birds' eggs, a broken rush chair, a doll's house, some old prints and boxes of Hudson's Dry Soap. Every English house may have one such room. Calke is composed almost entirely of them.

I first visited Calke in 1984 when its fate hung in the balance. The last Harpur Crewe was living there alone after inheriting the estate in 1981 from his brother, along with £8m of death duties. He had barely a penny in the world. The house lay lost in a fold of a large deer park in the Derbyshire hills. Its stone walls were crumbling. The interior was one huge family attic, filled with paraphernalia that successive members of the family had rejected and no auctioneer would take. What was to be done?

Calke was widely described as a time warp, mainly because the arrival of a telephone and some limited electricity had to await the 1960s. To me, it was not a time warp, just a house badly in need of a visit from the dustman. Yet within a year, Calke had been saved by the National Trust with money from every quarter. The National Trust went mad. Every tonic bottle, every match box, every chipped cup and broken chair was catalogued, dusted, wrapped in plastic and stored before being put back exactly where it had been in 1984. Nothing – or rather everything – was to be disturbed. A giant pretence was that the house was asleep. Apart from one object of which more below, it now contains three centuries of what might be anyone's junk.

Above Once the Great Hall, the saloon took on its present appearance during the time of Sir John Harpur Crewe, who owned Calke from 1844 to 1886. As he added more and more display cases, the room came to resemble a private museum of natural history. **Near right** The drawing room is just as full of family possessions; exotic stuffed birds and Meissen figurines, displayed under glass domes, stand on a late 18th-century satinwood commode.

The house was built in 1701–3 round the courtyard of an earlier Elizabethan mansion. The architect is unknown, although Calke has features in common with houses by the Smiths of Warwick. The exterior is in warm Derbyshire stone, well proportioned and free of surrounding outbuildings. There are acres of empty grass, and then a house. A hundred years after construction, an external staircase to the present saloon was removed and a formal Ionic portico inserted. The exotic Corinthian pilasters on the corner pavilions survive.

The entrance is now into the ground or 'rustic' floor, its hall dominated by trophies of the Harpur Crewes' prize cattle. Next door is the Caricature Room, which used to be thick with cobwebs. Georgian cartoons are pasted on the wall, some of them three layers deep.

The main saloon is English Baroque in style but dominated by glass cases of stuffed birds and animals, including a crocodile's head, set round a billiard table. The room served as a chapel in the 19th century, when the weather was too bad for the household to get to church. The drawing room and library have more character, if only by virtue of being crammed solid with things.

Above The low-ceilinged entrance hall is hung with heads of long-horned cattle, prize-winners bred on the estate at Calke that have stared down from these walls since the mid-19th century. **Below** The Boudoir was once a private sitting room, part of the principal suite of personal rooms at Calke. In 1821 Sir George Crewe, the 8th Baronet, adapted the suite and the sitting room became his wife's boudoir; it has changed little since this time.

Above The walls of the Caricature Room are pasted with cartoons in a variation on the traditional print room. **Right** None of the family rooms at Calke, except the saloon, were tall enough to accommodate the State Bed, which may explain why it was never put up in the house.

Three other rooms merit particular attention. On the second floor the Bird Lobby, cleansed of all mustiness and dirt, is astonishing for the sheer weight of taxidermy. The Gardner Wilkinson Library is my favourite, a dark cell of antiquarian books given to the family by an Egyptologist of that name in the 19th century. Then there is the Calke bed.

The historian, Sir Howard Colvin, was rummaging about Calke in the early 1980s when he stumbled on some unopened packing cases. The contents are thought to be a present to Lady Caroline Manners from George II's daughter, Princess Anne, for acting as bridesmaid at her wedding in 1734. The bed-hangings of imported Chinese silk had never been unpacked. The embroidery colours were as vivid as the day they was created. The hangings (c1715), have now been put on a frame and are a unique survival of 18th-century silk embroidery in such pristine condition. Peacocks and mandarins, animals and Chinese pagodas fill every inch of the surface. The bed was displayed at the Treasures of Britain exhibition in Washington in 1985 and is now protected behind glass.

The great park at Calke is as much a survivor as the house. Acquired to protect the inhabitants from any passing intrusion, it comprises woodland largely untended over three centuries. It is an ecological paradise.

Carnfield hall

★ ★ Atmospheric house, crammed with curios

Near Alfreton, 9 miles SE of Matlock; private house, open by arrangement

Carnfield is a miniature Calke. The story of the building is common, an Elizabethan manor flanked by Jacobean extensions, then 'turned' and given a new façade in the late 17th century. It is jolly rather than grand. Owned by the Revell family, it decayed over the centuries until being bought as derelict in 1987 by the present owner, James Cartland, antiques guru, broadcaster and conservationist.

Every room is crammed from floor to ceiling with the product of a lifetime's collecting, a reminder of Dickens' Golden Dustman in *Our Mutual Friend*. Not an inch is empty of objects. It hardly matters what purpose each room once served. Everywhere is the same mix of firearms, stuffed animals, piles of crockery, paintings of former owners, archives, silhouettes, historic costumes, gems and junk. There are books everywhere, mostly dusty and leathery and looking as if they have been there since Caxton.

Some of the rooms have distinguishing features. The hall has a Jacobean overmantel. The main stairs have newel posts and balusters of yeoman robustness. The Great Chamber over the hall is panelled and has a plaster frieze. Heavy curtains keep out the light and suggest that a squadron of bats may at any moment descend from the gloom.

In the many bedrooms, clothes and drapes conceal original timber and plaster partitions. Exotic feathers still adorn the four bed-posts in the master bedroom. An ante-room has been fashioned from what appears to be a minstrels' gallery. A stuffed badger guards one door, a musket another.

A visitor nurtured on Chatsworth asked Cartland, 'What is it all for, just what is it all for?' He could only shrug. Such houses are not 'for' anything at all. They are merely more precious than a dozen stately homes.

Catton hall

⭐ ⭐ Smith of Warwick house with fine interiors

8 miles SW of Burton-upon-Trent; private house, open by arrangement

Catton has been occupied by the same family, the Hortons then Neilsons, since the early 15th century. It was the bigamous marriage of an 18th-century Miss Horton – who had, according to Walpole, 'the most amorous eyes in the world' – to the brother of George III that reputedly led to the Royal Marriages Act. This prevented anyone in line to the throne from marrying without the Sovereign's consent.

The house has an outward plainness concealing a rich interior, a sedate lady burning with inner passion. From a distance across the park, the house looks almost modern, a redbrick box of nine bays, with windows diminishing in size on each floor and with only white keystones for adornment. The house was begun by James Gibbs but executed in 1745 by the younger Smith of Warwick, William, a new entrance being built to one side in 1829.

The finest interior is the former Great Hall, now the dining room. This has pronounced beams enriched with classical mouldings. The walls have Rococo plasterwork, musical trophies and classical doorcases. The drawing room beyond is more modest, with gilded beading to the wall panels and eagle candelabra holders. The house has fine pictures, including Stuart portraits and a Wright of Derby.

The Neilsons run the Catton estate on rigorously commercial principles, remarking that they can make more money from the house and lawn than from the whole of their farming estate. This is a stately home open for business. It is the future for many such houses.

Chatsworth

★★★★☆ Ducal palace set in landscaped parkland

Near Edensor, 7 miles NW of Matlock; private house, open part year

Chatsworth is, above all, a house in a landscape. It lies on the slope of a valley against a backdrop of wooded hills. I have seen it blazing golden in an autumn sunset, or rising serene above a spring mist. Floodlit at night, it appears like a luxury liner sliding quietly down its valley. In any mood, Chatsworth is spectacular. Yet it defers to the landscape. It does not shout, like Blenheim, or roar like Castle Howard.

The house is another creation of Bess of Hardwick. It came into her ownership through her marriage to Sir William Cavendish, father of her only children, and has passed down the Cavendish line ever since. The house was used by Bess's last husband, the Earl of Shrewsbury, to incarcerate Mary Queen of Scots, and was then rebuilt during the 1690s. The occasion was the elevation of the 1st Duke of Devonshire for his part in the Glorious Revolution. The Cavendishes have always been Whigs or Liberals (and even Social Democrats).

The house is no longer owned directly by the family. Devastating death duties in 1950 led to its transfer in perpetuity to an independent trust. But the family rent part of the house and the Duke and Duchess play a leading part in its management. Chatsworth pioneered this form of arm's-length preservation, keeping a house intact yet linked to the family. Accessibility has been traditional since the 17th century. In 1844 the house was open every day in the year, Sundays not excepted.

Instructions were that 'The humblest individual is not only shown the whole but the Duke has expressly ordered the waterworks to be played for everyone.' In the 1850s, with the coming of the railway, Chatsworth received 80,000 visitors a year.

Entrance from the road is down a winding drive that displays the main façade to best advantage. This front, of 1700–3, was built after the 1st Duke had quarrelled with William Talman, who had designed the south front to the right. Talman was Christopher Wren's rival in the Office of Works. Wren was a Tory and Talman a Whig. To the purist, the exterior of Chatsworth is rough and provincial, its orders truncated and resting on a bare ground floor. The glory of its exterior derived from its scale.

This glory was enhanced with the arrival in the 1760s of Capability Brown. He landscaped the River Derwent and tamed the rough pasture and hillside. Further changes occurred in the early 19th century when the 6th 'Bachelor' Duke converted Chatsworth from great house to palace. He removed the old village of Edensor from view and had Joseph Paxton install greenhouses and a gigantic fountain beneath the great cascade behind the house. Jeffry Wyatville was commissioned to build the extensive north wing, including a belvedere, theatre, sculpture gallery and grand dining room. It is next to this wing that the public enters the house.

The hall leads into the north corridor with its coloured marble pavement, a prelude to the majestic Painted Hall. Much altered over the years, this hall is the heart of Chatsworth. It retains the

'In any mood, Chatsworth is spectacular.'

ceiling painted for the original building of 1699 by Laguerre, depicting the triumphs of Julius Caesar, supposed precursor of William III as champion of English liberty. The staircase rises through a magnificent screen to a landing. Half hidden beyond is another staircase, with metalwork balustrades by Jean Tijou, rising to the state rooms, as if one grand stair is not enough for Chatsworth. The walls are decorated with grisaille panels and the niches filled with statues by Colley Cibber. On the landings is a set of old baby-carriages, a child's Rococo sleigh beautifully crafted.

The state rooms at Chatsworth are unusually on the second floor, behind Talman's south front. The reason for this arrangement is not clear. The family rooms are below and the assumption is that the 1st Duke decided to convert into state rooms an upper Long Gallery surviving from the earlier Tudor house. Hardwick's most formal rooms were – and are – on the top floor. The 6th Duke later referred to them as his 'dismal, ponderous range of Hampton Court-like chambers'. When the house was a girls' school during the Second World War, these rooms were dormitories, surely the most splendid in the land.

Left Chatsworth is entered through the North Front Hall, the kitchen of the house until the 1760s. The original ranges are still *in situ*, concealed behind the fireplaces. **Below** The ceiling and upper walls of the Painted Hall have remained unchanged since they were decorated in the 1690s. The stairs, however, have been subject to several alterations. In 1833 Sir Jeffry Wyatville changed the original twin curved stairs to a single flight and added two galleries along the walls. These were demolished and replaced with the current stairs and single gallery in 1912.

Above The walls of the state music room are covered with stamped and gilded leather, hung here in the 1830s by the 6th Duke after he had seen similar decoration at Fontainebleau. **Right** In the state bedchamber the 6th Duke's leather wall-hangings have been covered with Brussels tapestries to re-create the late 17th-century style decor that would have been chosen by the 1st Duke. A 28-piece silver-gilt toilet service is on display, a gift to the 1st Duchess from Queen Mary II.

Restoration has made them less dismal. They are merely magnificent. The state dining room, in which it is said that nobody has ever dined, has a ceiling by Verrio. It includes the 1st Duke's housekeeper, Mrs Hackett, whom Verrio did not like, 'cutting the thread of life' with scissors. The sumptuous wood carving is 'school of Gibbons' and some of the furniture is by William Kent. The state drawing room contains a set of Mortlake tapestries, copied from the Raphael cartoons now in the V&A, and another ceiling by Laguerre. The state music room has a *trompe-l'œil* violin painted on its door. The stamped leather wall-hangings, introduced *c*1830, are anachronistic and exotic; in the 1690s the walls were covered in green velvet. Viewing this room is like eating an over-rich box of chocolates. The state bedchamber follows, its 18th-century damask-hung bed is said to have been the death-bed of George II. The last in the sequence, the state dressing room, enjoys the finest views, both south and west.

The route now enters the 19th century, with corridors and stairs added to the central courtyard by Wyatville for the 6th Duke. In the Sketch Gallery are portraits of the family and more Mortlake tapestries, while the west staircase includes paintings acquired by successive dukes, from Tintoretto to Lucien Freud.

The chapel survives from the 1st Duke's rebuild. Its superb alabaster reredos contains Verrio's *Doubting Thomas* over the altar and carvings by Gibbons and others. The eccentric Oak Room beyond was acquired by the 6th Duke from dealers who looted Continental monasteries in the 1820s and 1830s. It has twisted columns forming a sort of sanctuary in the middle and was used as a smoking room.

'It is **hard to convey** the
sheer richness of this place.'

Above When the 6th Duke created his library from the former Long Gallery in around 1815 he kept the gilded stucco ceiling with its paintings by Verrio. An Axminster carpet, made for the new room, was designed to reflect the roundels in the ceiling. The bookcases and upper gallery were designed by the Duke and his architect Wyatville in the 1830s.

The route passes back through the Painted Hall and climbs to the libraries via the Oak Stairs, with its antler chandelier and Grinling Gibbons' limewood cravat. Here begins what amounts to a second Chatsworth, the Regency wing designed by Wyatville for the 6th Duke. The 1st Duke's Long Gallery was converted into the first of three libraries. It contains what is still England's finest book collection in private hands, although it is only a fragment of that owned by the family in the 19th century. Death duties saw the loss to America of the Caxtons and Shakespeare First Folios. It was perhaps a fitting transference of old wealth to new, but a great loss to Chatsworth.

The 19th-century house in no way outguns the 17th century, but it reaches a sort of climax in Wyatville's Great Dining Room. Here the Bachelor Duke came into his own, describing eating here as 'like dining in a great trunk, and you expect the lid to open'. Here are paintings by van Dyck and Mytens, and the Gainsborough of Georgiana, Duchess of Devonshire, acquired by Chatsworth in 1994. Beyond are more paintings and sculpture in the gallery, arranged as a homage to Canova and to Regency taste generally. It is hard to convey the sheer richness of this place. It is the National Gallery of the North and yet a home.

Chesterfield: Revolution house

⭐ Ancient cottage and scene of historic meeting

High Street, Old Whittington, Chesterfield; museum, open part year

Hardly a house but certainly historic, Revolution House was the venue of a seminal meeting in English history. Here, in 1688, a group of men took shelter from the rain when out hunting on Whittington Moor. The hunt had an ulterior motive. The Earl of Danby, the Earl of Devonshire and John D'Arcy came to plan the overthrow of James II and the invitation to William of Orange to invade and seize the throne. They thus initiated the Glorious Revolution – and a dukedom for Devonshire. The building was then an inn, the Cock and Pynot, which later became a farmhouse.

A place of pilgrimage for those honouring Parliamentary democracy, the house stands by a green in a suburb of Chesterfield. It is a precious survivor of an ancient Derbyshire farm building. Stone walls support a thick thatch roof. A single dormer window lights a small upper chamber. There are just two rooms downstairs, with 17th-century furniture and a smattering of material about the origins of the 1688 meeting. The only intrusion is a video.

Derby: Pickford's house

⭐ Georgian architect's house, now a museum of costume

Friar Gate, Derby; museum, open all year

Friar Gate is a precious fragment of old Derby. Its finest building is Pickford's House, built in 1769 by a local architect, Joseph Pickford. The façade is classical, pedimented and with a Doric doorcase surmounted by the tools of the architect's profession. Why cannot modern architecture use these same tools to produce streetscapes of similar grace?

The house is now a museum of mostly Regency costumes. The rooms are shuttered and lights come on when visitors enter. This is conservation gone mad, stripping the interior of all atmosphere and confining visitors to glass cages in each of the main rooms, like zoo animals.

The front hall has fine plasterwork, a sign of wealth in a town house. The main reception rooms on the ground floor are laid out by time of day. The drawing room is for tea, the dining room for dessert and the morning room 'light and airy' for the ladies, though in reality gloomy. The street outside is respectably Georgian and there is no good reason for not opening the curtains to the view.

Upstairs, the house relaxes a little. The 1930s bathroom is 'for public use', a nice touch. A bedroom is prepared for cocoa-time, with the bed linen turned down and nightshirts laid ready. The remainder of the house is an exhibition of display cases.

Eyam hall

Left The hangings that line the Tapestry Room are said to have come from Bradshaw Hall in Eyam, a once-grand house, now ruined. At the centre of one wall is a 16th-century Brussels tapestry that depicts an Old Testament scene; Jehu, seen dressed as a Roman soldier, is being crowned with a laurel wreath.

★ ★ Seventeenth-century mansion built in Elizabethan style

At Eyam, 10 miles NW of Buxton; private house, open part year

The village of Eyam is famous for its heroism during the Plague of 1665-6, when the village was infected by cloth from London and sealed itself off from the world until the plague had passed. Half its people died. There are many relics of those days in the village, but not in Eyam Hall, whose story begins with its purchase and rebuilding by Thomas Wright in 1671. His descendants live in the house to this day. Eyam is a delightfully romantic place, Restoration in date but Jacobean, if not Elizabethan, in appearance. The façade, with its blank wall above the front door and austere gable ends, looks a hundred years older than its date.

The interior is a rich sequence of 17th-century rooms, very much in family use and crammed with Wright memorabilia. A painting in the entrance hall celebrates the auspicious marriage of John Wright to the girl in the picture, Elizabeth Kniveton, a picture of Derbyshire respectability. By the hall fire are two rare 'bacon' settles, seats with cupboards in their backs for hanging hams to cure near the fire.

The main rooms are upstairs. A Tapestry Room is entirely covered in the material, cut to fit even the window openings and door surrounds as if it were wallpaper. One part is made of a valuable 15th-century piece from Flanders. The library was the old Great Chamber, a place of creaking floors and heavy bookshelves. A 17th-century 'pop-up' medical encyclopaedia is on display. Engraved in the window is a passionate love poem written by Robert Wright in the 18th century. It is dedicated to Fanny Holme of Stockport. He married twice but never to Fanny, yet the window survived.

The bedroom has a magnificent four-poster and a delightful portrait of a Wright girl in a hat. Eyam is blessed with a complete run of such pictures, none great works of art but full of local charm, one English family in continuous narrative. Many of the 17th-century works came through John Wright's marriage to Jane Farewell who brought her own collection with her. To these are added more modern photographs from the Victorian age to today.

Haddon hall

★★★★☆ Medieval fortified hall house set around a courtyard

Near Bakewell, 5 miles NW of Matlock; private house, open part year

Haddon is the most perfect English house to survive from the Middle Ages. It has none of Hardwick's promiscuity or Chatsworth's bombast. It has not changed because it never needed to change. From the 15th century to today, this cluster of warm stone buildings has lain in its valley, protected by a curtain wall and surrounding forest. Those aristocratic curses of extravagance and infertility have not visited Haddon. The place is still owned by the Manners family, Dukes of Rutland. To wander up the slope to the worn gatehouse steps and enter the ancient courtyard is as agreeable an experience as England can offer.

Haddon was the seat of Sir George Vernon, 'King of the Peak', having been in his line since 1170. It passed to the Manners family after Vernon's daughter, Dorothy, allegedly raced from her sister's wedding feast and eloped with John Manners, son

'It has **not changed** because it **never needed** to change.'

Above The Long Gallery at Haddon was created at the end of the 16th century by Sir John Manners and his wife, Dorothy, who had inherited the Hall on the death of her father, Sir George Vernon, in 1565. The Gallery, some 110 feet long, is lined with carved oak panelling that was originally limewashed and then painted with designs in a rusty red colour.

of the Earl of Rutland, in 1563. The houses of Belvoir and Haddon were thus united in one family and have remained so ever since. Through the 18th and 19th centuries, the Rutlands neglected Haddon in favour of their seat of Belvoir, in Leicestershire. This saved it from the drastic alterations that occurred to most houses over that period. Haddon's restoration by the 9th Duke after 1912 and recently by his grandson have been deferential.

The approach to the house is without pretension. The visitor is greeted not by a grand gateway but by an old Tudor stable block. In the adjacent garden is a topiary hedge, clipped to display a boar's head and a peacock, emblems respectively of Vernon and Manners. Up the slope to the right lies a rough medieval gatehouse with modest armorial dressings. Above it are the rooms in which the 9th Duke slept while supervising the 20th-century restoration.

The Lower Courtyard holds the essence of Haddon. It is that of a fortified house rather than castle, yet with none of the tight enclosure of Berkeley, in Gloucestershire, or Skipton, in Yorkshire. The hall, solar, chapel, kitchens and offices lie low and comfortable round an open court which for centuries echoed to the clatter of horses and the shouts of visitors.

The Great Hall at Haddon is small, almost square in plan and dated *c*1370. The roof is a modern restoration, but the original screens passage, minstrels' gallery, dais and panelling survive. The antlers are 17th century and the dais tapestry was reputedly given to a Manners by Henry VIII. On the screen

is a manacle for those 'who did not drink fayre'. Haddon's kitchens are extensive, a warren of pantry, buttery, bakery and courtyard. The survival of their furnishings, including salting baths, chopping boards, log boxes and baking ovens we owe to centuries of disuse.

At the other end of the Great Hall are the original family rooms, which developed round the solar. They are among the finest to survive intact from the 15th century. The original Great Chamber was divided into dining room and receiving room. The dining room has a painted ceiling depicting the Tudor rose and emblems of the Vernon and Talbot families. A frieze above the panelling continues the heraldic theme, a cartoon strip of the great figures of the day. The plan of this room is repeated in the Great Chamber above.

Next come the Earl's Apartments, domestic rooms once sub-divided for warmth and privacy. Heavy oak ceilings and floorboards are left exposed and whitewash liberally applied. The windows offer delicious glimpses of the Haddon gardens on the slopes below.

The Upper Courtyard remains mostly private to the family. Its rooms met the Elizabethan need for large entertaining spaces, before the move to Belvoir. The Long Gallery is not as spectacular as that at Hardwick. It is lit by three tiers of Elizabethan windows, the panes set at differing angles to pattern

Left The Great Hall at Haddon became known as the Banqueting Hall some time after the 15th century when the Vernons began to spend more time in their private chambers in the solar wing and the hall came to be set aside as a room for entertainment. **Below** The south wall of the chapel is decorated with a design of leaves and flowers. These and other wall paintings were probably executed in the early 15th century but by the Reformation they had been plastered over and were only uncovered again during the 9th Duke's restoration work of the early 20th century.

Above The Great Chamber as it appears today was created around 1500; the plasterwork ceiling in the oriel bay, however, was added during the 17th century. The oak panelling dates from around the same time and was once highly decorated; remains of gold and green paint can still be seen.

the fall of light onto the interior, a device I have seen nowhere else; it was possibly inserted during 20th-century restoration. The oak panelling celebrates the Vernon-Manners union and the reign of James I, with boars and peacocks united with roses and thistles. Over the mantelpiece is a charming Rex Whistler painting of Haddon, commissioned in honour of the 20th-century restoration.

Beyond is the state bedroom with its ante-chamber. Both are used to display tapestries, including the 'Sense' of smell from the Mortlake workshop. A Brussels tapestry shows a horse treading on the foot of a pike-bearer. Over the mantelpiece is a crowded tableau of Orpheus charming the beasts, with the Manners peacock taking precedence over monkeys and elephants. Haddon's state bed is sadly at Belvoir, encased in a glass box and thus a museum piece, not a bed. It should be brought back and left to fade gracefully in its proper home.

The old chapel contains Norman masonry and medieval wall paintings. Its oak pews are graded for the family and servants. The Haddon gardens are a story in themselves. They cascade down the hillside from the curtain wall towards the river, terraced by the Duchess while her husband restored the house.

Hardwick hall

★★★★☆ The greatest English prodigy house of the Elizabethan era

10 miles E of Matlock; National Trust, open part year

The spectacle of Hardwick Hall, gold and shimmering in the setting sun, is one of the most splendid in English architecture. It was Bess of Hardwick's final assertion of independence from her husband, the 6th Earl of Shrewsbury (see Hardwick Old Hall, page 84). The initials ES woven fourteen times into its parapet have even been claimed for female emancipation. The building was regarded as the highpoint of the Elizabethan 'Renaissance', yet Hardwick seems a place apart. Like Bolsover, it was built for a game of manners whose rules have largely vanished. It is now architecture as abstract sculpture, four walls of glass entombing light. Turrets, chambers, stairs and the incomparable upper gallery stand sentinel over a steep valley. Hardwick is never less than sad.

The house was begun on Shrewsbury's death in 1590 probably to designs by Robert Smythson, who was already working at Wollaton, in Nottinghamshire. Hardwick was the more

'Hardwick was **for show. It was meant to make men gasp.'**

Above left The Great Hall bears the Hardwick coat of arms, carved into the plasterwork overmantel. The arms are supported by two stags, each bearing real antlers. **Above right** Bess of Hardwick would have received important visitors in the High Great Chamber, enthroned beneath a sumptuous canopy; the example on display today was made in the 1620s for the wife of her grandson, the 2nd Earl of Devonshire. **Left** A portrait of Mary, Queen of Scots and her husband, Lord Darnley, hangs at Hardwick: Bess's fourth husband, the Earl of Shrewsbury, was entrusted with guarding the Queen from 1569 until 1584.

accomplished work, both in the perfection of its proportion and in its use of the defining material of Elizabethan wealth, glass. It was the secular answer to the great Perpendicular churches of the previous century. Hardwick was for show. It was meant to make men gasp.

The celebrated entrance front is a mirror of the seasons, lowering and grim in cloud, a flickering façade of colour in sun. The walk round the outside of Hardwick shows its walls shifting and rearranging themselves before the eye. Each side seems different, each sailing along in a different wind. The side elevations are tall and slender, like the prow of a galleon surging through the sea. The historian Olive Cook watched 'the immense diamond window panes flash and vibrate with a hundred molten colours'.

The house is unaltered. As at the Old Hall the Great Hall is aligned front-to-back, dividing the house into equal sides. The ground floor is for services, with pantry and kitchen on either side of the Hall. The family rooms are on the taller first floor. Taller still is the second floor, the place of entertainment and display, as if greatness lay in height and the suspense of achieving it. The exterior is fractured by six towers crowned with six pavilions, lending each floor angles of constant visual diversion. Stairs extend into towers, forming landings and private closets. On the upper floors the towers produce L-shaped, E-shaped and T-shaped chambers, all flooded with light.

Hardwick is a house of staircases, two of which thread their way through all the floors. The Great Stair rises between heavy tapestries to Bess's Low Great Chamber, linked by a bridge over the end of the hall to her withdrawing room. These chambers have glorious mantelpieces and panelling, with furniture returned over the past century from Chatsworth and elsewhere. The withdrawing room was the sitting room of the last occupant of the house, Evelyn, Duchess of Devonshire, who died in 1960. It displays Elizabethan and later embroidery, including works by Bess.

We are constantly drawn back to the stairs. The wide, flowing curve of steps to the top floor is like the approach to the chapter house at Wells. Tapestries now trumpet the approach to greatness. The High Great Chamber and Long Gallery at Hardwick are sumptuous rooms. They seem double the height of the floor below. The chamber is lined with Brussels tapestries of Ulysses beneath a coloured plaster frieze of the Hunt of Diana. They surround a Serlian fireplace of marble and alabaster. Pevsner is snooty about much of this. A visitor from Fontainebleau or Florence, he said, would have found it 'a monstrous show ... barbaric in the extreme'. I prefer to see it as an outburst of confident northern vigour.

The withdrawing room next door contains the finest Elizabethan furniture in the house. Here stands a beautiful marquetry chest. Even Pevsner's foreigners would have admired the exquisite bas relief of Apollo and the Muses.

The Long Gallery is the apotheosis of Elizabethan architecture. The room is E-shaped, the outer wall of three bays, one shallow, two deep, filled with glass. The inner walls are lined with tapestries and 81 portraits, including one of hard-faced Bess. But this is a room not of objects but of stone framing space and light. On a sunny day it is an avenue ablaze. On a dark one it revives a belief in ghosts. After this Gallery, the remainder of Hardwick is anticlimax.

Left The Green Velvet Room gets its name from the 18th-century bed and matching chairs brought to Hardwick from Londesborough by the 6th Duke of Devonshire in the early 19th century. **Above** The 6th Duke also introduced the magnificent canopy that stands in the Long Gallery. This was originally the tester and head of Chatsworth's state bed, made in 1697. **Right** A portrait of Bess in her seventies hangs in the Long Gallery. Dressed simply in a widow's black, she wears the 'fore ropes of great perle' described in a 1593 inventory of her jewellery.

Hardwick Old hall

★★ The remains of Bess of Hardwick's old mansion

10 miles E of Matlock; English Heritage, open part year

The ghost of Elizabeth Shrewsbury haunts the hills of Derbyshire. Born in 1527, 'Bess of Hardwick' saw out the 16th century, dying in 1608 shortly after the monarch whose name she shared. She was never Good Queen Bess. She was no aristocrat, although she founded whole dynasties of them, but came of Derbyshire yeoman stock. Bess was a hard, acquisitive, upwardly mobile Elizabethan. She found wealth through her husbands, four of them. No alimony scrounger is her equal. The two houses at Hardwick are her memorial.

Bess was married at fourteen, widowed at fifteen, then married again to the wealthy Sir William Cavendish, by whom she had eight children. He died and she remarried at thirty. Widowed a third time, she then married the richest man in England, the Earl of Shrewsbury. The marriage was bitterly unhappy. The matrimonial wars of the Shrewsburys lent 'shrew' to the language. They were so ferocious that the Queen herself had to act as conciliator, unsuccessfully. The Earl declared that 'no plague' was as evil as his wife. Even her admirers found Bess 'of masculine understanding and conduct, proud, furious, selfish and unfeeling ... hideous, dry, parched, narrow-minded'.

Yet Bess's lineage was to embrace the dukedoms of Devonshire, Newcastle, Portland, Kingston and Norfolk. In her own lifetime, her family houses included Chatsworth, Hardwick, Bolsover, Oldcotes, Sheffield, Welbeck and Worksop, among others. She was a fanatical architect. After Shrewsbury's death in 1590, a fortune teller (doubtless a builder) prophesied that Bess 'should not die while she was building'. She eventually died in the fierce winter of 1607–8 when cold had briefly halted work on her new hall at Hardwick.

Bess had been born in the Old Hall and it was to here that she returned after her separation from Shrewsbury in 1584. She began to extend the old house three years later, even as she was planning her new Hall opposite. The older building was thus a piecemeal structure, with ranges

'Even centuries of decay cannot wipe the tear from its face.'

and grand rooms added when needed. Part was used by her favourite son, William Cavendish, for his own establishment. Between them, they had some 200 retainers. The new Hall would be for ostentation, entertainment and special guests. The Old Hall was for Bess, her family and entourage.

When the later Cavendishes rebuilt Chatsworth and made it their seat, Hardwick lost its pre-eminence. The Old Hall was partly dismantled and its fittings distributed to various family properties. It was left a ruin and by the 19th century was already the object of antiquarian interest. In 1959 it was given to the nation by the 10th Duke of Devonshire in lieu of death duties. The new Hardwick Hall opposite passed to the National Trust.

The ruin is that which Bess left, unaltered. The entrance leads into what became an 'end-on' Great Hall, running front-to-back and dividing the old service rooms to the right from the family chambers to the left. By the late 16th century, the Great Hall was no longer a dining room, more an entrance and servants' hall. Yet as Bess built, so the house divided into what was her wing on one side and her son's on the other. This produced not one but two formal suites, the Hill Great Chamber and the Forest Great Chamber. They were built high, four floors up, the extravagant stairs designed to impress visitors. The apartments were equalled in scale only by royal palaces.

Of these apartments, only fragments survive. The decoration of the Forest Chamber depicted the deer of the woods, a metaphor for Bess waiting patiently for her husband to return to her, as she wanted it thought. Off the staircase are rooms known to have been allocated to two senior servants, Mr Digby and Mr Reason, each with plaster panels. The Hill Great Chamber overlooks the valley, with windows on three sides. Its overmantel still displays reliefs of Gog and Magog, hence its nickname of the Giants' Chamber.

The Old Hall at Hardwick, although ruined, is somehow more real than the new one. It developed in response to domestic need and tells a human story. It was not just a show house but the residence of a dysfunctional family. Even centuries of decay cannot wipe the tear from its face.

Kedleston hall

✦ ✦ ✦ ✦ Adam's re-creation of grand imperial Roman villa

5 miles NW of Derby; National Trust, open part year

What is to be made of Kedleston? Curzons came over at the Norman Conquest and have been in residence ever since. They represented their county in Parliament and their monarch in India. Here, in the soft foothills of the Peak District, they created a house in the grandest Roman style, employing the most inventive architect of the day, Robert Adam. They preserved his masterpiece and in 1986 handed it intact to the National Trust.

Yet there is something frigid about this house. It seems to spring perfect from Adam's pattern book without human intervention. The family have lived only in the lower floor and in the north-east pavilion; the main rooms were for entertaining and showing to the public. Walking through these rooms I feel Hogarth's longing for English roast beef. Dr Johnson wrote that it 'would do excellently for a Town Hall'. We seem to bruise Kedleston by our very presence.

The façade unfolds from the landscape like a golden summons. It was commissioned by the 5th Baronet, Sir Nathaniel Curzon (later 1st Lord Scarsdale), on his inheritance in 1758. An exquisite young man of thirty-two who had missed out on the Grand Tour, Curzon wanted a house in the height of fashion.

'The façade unfolds from the landscape like a golden summons.'

Right Adam designed the Saloon at Kedleston to be equivalent to the *vestibulum* of a Roman villa, a room where images of the gods were venerated. The alcoves around the room, therefore, were originally home to suitable statues. These, however, were moved to the Marble Hall next door in 1788 and replaced with urns on plinths. Above the doorways are landscapes of Roman ruins by William Hamilton; above the alcoves are scenes from English medieval history, painted in grisaille by Biagio Rebecca.

'Grant me, ye Gods, a pleasant seat,' he wrote, 'in Attick elegance made neat.' He tried Matthew Brettingham and James Paine, who between them built the two wing houses. But on meeting Robert Adam, recently returned from the Mediterranean, Curzon was 'struck all of a heap with wonder and amaze'. A Tory, he wanted to outdo the Whig Cavendishes at Chatsworth. The glories of ancient Rome would now be reborn on the slopes of Derbyshire. Adam, in turn, was delighted to find a client 'resolved to spare no expense, with £10,000 a year ... a taste for the Arts and little for game'.

Adam did not take over full responsibility for Kedleston until 1760. He accepted the Brettingham/Paine Palladian front but added a façade of his own to the rear, a variant on the Arch of Constantine with steps curving down to the garden. Whereas the front is severely Palladian, the rear is an echo of Vanbrugh. That was the limit of Adam's exterior alterations. Even Curzon soon ran out of money and the original plan, for four pavilions linked by curving quadrants, as at Holkham Hall, in Norfolk, was not realized.

'It is the atrium of a Roman villa ...'

The decoration is from Adam's sketchbooks and notebooks. No civilization has paid a greater compliment to another than was paid by Georgian England to Rome. But whereas the Palladians of the Burlington School drew on the heavier tradition of the Italian Renaissance, Adam reverted to the Roman Empire itself. His tendrils, arabesques and acanthus leaves framing classical medallions were drawn from the Emperor Diocletian's recently unearthed palace in Split. This was a lighter, more delicate, and almost frivolous, revival.

The interiors at Kedleston are almost all by Adam, designed for the grandest of show. A central hall and saloon cross the centre of the building, with the family rooms to the left and state rooms to the right. They form a compact quadrilateral parade. The Marble Hall is entered directly from the flight of steps under the front portico. It is the atrium of a Roman villa, top lit and with no windows. The walls are lined with 20 columns, behind which are statue niches with relief panels above. All depict scenes from classical antiquity. The coving of the ceiling is by Adam's plasterer, Joseph Rose. Even the iron grates and fire irons are by Adam.

The promenade begins on the left with the music room, the only ceremonial room still regularly used by the family. Beyond lies the drawing room, in part designed by Paine before Adam's arrival. Its centrepiece is a marble Venetian window balanced by marble doorcases, two of them false. The ceiling coving by Joseph Rose contains a wild naturalistic composition, like waves frothing over the frieze. The walls are lined with four superb sofas by John Linnell, made in London in 1765 and glories of English 18th-century

craftsmanship. The mermaids on the arms invite us to lie down and relax. (Do no such thing: this is the National Trust.)

The library beyond is a haven of sudden calm. The ceiling is patterned on geometric mosaics from Rome and Ravenna. The classical orders are no longer Corinthian but Doric, the books immaculate in their glass-fronted cases. The corner to the rear front now turns into the circular saloon. This is a sensational chamber based on the Pantheon. The ceiling is a dazzling *trompe-l'œil* of rosettes disappearing upwards to a central skylight, the niches likewise swirling to some notional vanishing point. When used as a ballroom, the effect on the dancers must have been intoxicating.

The state apartments on the other side of the hall begin with ante-rooms preparing the visitor for the state bedchamber. Its bed is not heavy like early 18th-century beds: the canopy is supported on posts carved as two slender palm trees, their roots growing from floorboards, rising up to waves of foliage. Ostrich feathers crown the composition. Palms were illustrative of victory, ostrich feathers of power. The bed is clothed in blue brocade, a masterpiece of English Rococo.

The circuit is completed by the dining room, with an apsidal niche at the kitchen end for the display of family silver. Adam was so emphatic about how pictures were hung at Kedleston that he even designed picture frames in plaster, requiring the paintings to be hung symmetrically. Below stairs, on the ground or 'rustic' floor, is the Caesar's Hall where normal life in the house continued while the rooms upstairs were mostly covered in dust sheets. Here, too, is Curzon's Museum, installed by the Marquess in honour of his time as Viceroy of India. It includes the celebrated 'peacock dress' worn by his wife at the 1903 Coronation Durbar in Delhi.

The grounds at Kedleston are rare for an 18th-century house in *not* being by Capability Brown, but by the architect of the house, in this case Adam himself. They are in the Brown style, naturalistic but adorned with Adam pavilions and even bath-houses for the use of visiting members of the public.

Left The columns that line the Marble Hall are made of alabaster quarried from the Nottinghamshire estate of Sir Nathaniel Curzon's brother. The floor is made of a local stone, from Hopton Wood, inlaid with white Italian marble. **Right** John Linnell created four sofas for the drawing room, based on an Adam design of 1762. They are carved with mermaids and sea gods, echoing the maritime theme of the room's decor. Sir Nathaniel collected model ships and had originally wanted the ceiling painted with scenes of British naval victories. Adam baulked at this but did include sea monsters and merfolk among the final plasterwork decoration.

Melbourne hall

★★☆ Jacobean and Georgian mansion

At Melbourne, 8 miles S of Derby;
private house, open part year

Melbourne is a church, house, garden and one lovely room. The church was the mini-cathedral built by the Bishops of Carlisle, reluctant to stray too far north to their headquarters and the threatening Scots. The house was later leased from the bishops and then rebuilt as a private house in 1629 by Sir John Coke. He was forebear of the Lambs and then Kerrs, the present owners.

A new west wing was added early in the 18th century, forming one side of a narrow three-sided courtyard to the south of Coke's house. The Jacobean Great Hall became the new dining room. In 1744, the house was further altered when the younger Smith of Warwick, William, added a handsome wing facing the garden. It has a rusticated ground floor and decorative swags in the central pediment, forming a fine backdrop to the sweep of the garden below.

The present interior is of two parts, one of 1629 and the other Georgian. The earlier is dominated by the dining room, superbly panelled and with family portraits by Huysmans, Jansens and Lely. The colourful heraldic overmantel is an import from a Kerr estate in Hertfordshire. With its pewter and high-backed embroidered chairs, the room embodies the style and comfort of an early 17th-century gentleman.

The staircase and hall are those of a conventional but not elaborate Georgian house. The stairwell has a moulded plaster ceiling. Smith's drawing room and study face the garden. All are hung with pictures tracing the ownership of the house from Cokes to Lambs, a lineage that embraced Lord Melbourne, Lady Caroline Lamb and Lord Palmerston. The Kerrs, Marquesses of Lothian, inherited the house in the 19th century. The present Lady Ralph Kerr, an artist, has added to the Melbourne collection with her own delightful paintings.

The gardens of Melbourne are not extensive but richly displayed. The main vista down to the pool is flanked by billowing waves of yew. Wooded glades are punctuated by van Nost statuary. In one glade is a charming arbour of swirling Italianate ironwork by Robert Blackwell of Derby.

Renishaw hall

★ ★ ☆ Gothicized Jacobean house with famous family collections

Near Renishaw, 8 miles SE of Sheffield; private house, open by arrangement

The Derbyshire Sitwells made their money from nails and coal. Their descendants could thus afford to be 20th-century aesthetes. In the decade after the Great War, the children of Sir George Sitwell, Osbert, Edith and Sacheverell, became, in the words of their biographer Anthony Powell, 'style-setters and standard-bearers in the war against the Philistines, heroes to a new generation of dandy writers'. Their domineering father had talent and taste. Their mother, Lady Ida, was 'irresponsible, sensual and extravagant'. To Powell they were 'tall, fair, attenuated courtiers from a medieval tapestry'. That is what nails can do for you.

Renishaw became famous and much visited by literary and artistic figures. Its ghosts were celebrated, terrifying even sceptical guests. They sometimes slapped faces and pushed people off stairs at night. The ghost of a drowned boy was said to give wet, cold kisses to sleeping ladies. There was more than a suspicion of practical joking in all this. The house is now owned by Sacheverell's son, Sir Reresby. It is as variegated and eccentric as the family's history.

Renishaw was built *c*1625 as a conventional Jacobean house, and gothicized at the turn of the 19th century. 'Renishaw cannot claim to be an architectural gem,' asserts the guidebook emphatically. Its exterior looks like that of an expensive prep school. The interior could not be less so. It bursts with the magpie zeal of generations of Sitwells. Two Venetian warriors in fancy dress adorn the front

Above The ballroom was added to Renishaw Hall in 1808 in order to hold a ball in honour of the Prince of Wales and his daughter, Princess Charlotte. It was designed by the Sheffield architect, Joseph Badger, who incorporated the three feathers of the Prince of Wales in the plasterwork decoration of the ceiling.

hall, one wearing spectacles left by a visitor in 1969 and still not reclaimed. Directly ahead is a large fireplace with an overmantel of Venice by a Renishaw regular, John Piper. Other Pipers line the walls.

The rooms adjacent to the hall retain their 17th-century proportions with Jacobean colours boldly restored. The Smoke Room is in bright red with yellow panelling. The ante-dining room is deep green, a perfect setting for the Dutch paintings. The dining room, added in 1793, is Adamish in style and soft pink in colour. It features a wide, handsome and practical apse for the sideboard and is dominated by two works, John Copley's conversation piece of the Sitwells in 1787 and a tremendous 17th-century Neapolitan cabinet, black and gold and covered in classical scenes.

The Regency wing contains the Great Drawing Room and ballroom. The atmosphere of these rooms could hardly be less Jacobean, more what Osbert Lancaster called 'Curzon Street Baroque'. They are a gallery of Sitwell acquisitions, English and Continental works tossed together in happy confusion. The floor of the drawing room was stained with a discreet

floral pattern in 1988. A Chippendale commode is companion to a superb piece at Harewood House and was, in Sacheverell Sitwell's opinion, 'the finer of the pair'. Above it hangs a Sargent painting of the Edwardian Sitwells.

Much of the charm of Renishaw is to experience English Jacobean shifting gear into Baroque. The Brussels tapestries in the drawing room, thankfully allowed to see the light of day, gave Sacheverell his enthusiasm for the 'suavity and opulence' of the then unfashionable Baroque. So too did the sumptuous ballroom, most of its contents Italian. Two giant dolphins rest on a marble table. Near it stands the largest vase of Derbyshire Bluejohn stone extant. Dominating the space, almost as an altarpiece, is Salvator Rosa's *Belisarius in Disgrace* in a frame attributed to William Kent. Renishaw does nothing by halves.

That certainly goes for the ravishing garden, largely the brainchild of the present owner's highly eccentric grandfather. It was he who was alleged to have gazed across the crowded industrial valley of Derbyshire at Barlborough on its bluff in the distance and remarked that 'there is no one between us and the Locker-Lampsons'.

Sudbury hall

★ ★ ★   Late 17th-century house with remarkable interiors

At Sudbury, 6 miles E of Uttoxeter; National Trust, open part year

The house belonged to a junior line of the Vernons of Haddon Hall. Having been abandoned by them in 1967, Sudbury passed to the National Trust with the best of intentions. The Trust created the best of museums, a cold, rather empty place but uplifted by one of England's finest staircases.

George Vernon inherited Sudbury in 1660 on the death of his father and rebuilt the house with a remarkably old-fashioned exterior for the time. The north and south façades are both E-plan, with diapered brickwork and large, stone-mullioned windows with some circular tracery. The porch is even odder, with two segmental arches, one above the other, filled with classical enrichment. The doorway in the lower arch seems to have sunk in despair below the bases of the attached columns. The composition is undeniably grand but this style was so imitated, and bloated, by 19th-century Jacobethans that it now looks rather institutional.

The inside is a different matter. The porch leads into a screens passage with a hall on the right. Over the fireplace is an uplifting Laguerre mural, Time offering a cornucopia to Industry and thorns to Idleness. But this hall is little more than an ante-chamber, giving way to Sudbury's masterpiece, the Great Staircase leading up to the promenade of Long Gallery and Queen's Room. The staircase, possibly designed by Vernon himself, is a flourish of 17th-century decoration. The carpenter was Wren's assistant, Edward Pierce. The plasterer was James Pettifer.

This is one of the great stairs of England and was, for once, by an Englishman. It rises in two shallow flights, its underside as richly decorated as its walls and ceiling. Most astonishing are Pierce's

upstairs reached from behind, an unsatisfactory arrangement. The saloon, though bare of furniture, is another virtuoso work by Pierce, with ceiling by Pettifer and his colleague, Robert Bradbury. Again, the room seems to drip with moulding and carving, palm leaves and acanthus enfolding nuts and fruit in a celebration of plenty. The wall panels frame full-length family portraits by Hudson, Dahl and others.

The drawing room beyond has, as its overmantel, one of the earliest documented carvings by Grinling Gibbons, of a bunch of fishes. They form an intriguing comparison with Pierce's work next door, in my view superior but a close call. The remaining rooms on the ground floor are more domestic, offering views out over the lake. Their redecoration by John Fowler in the 1970s was controversial but, as he countered at the time, such decoration is always 'a striving after a sense of life and not just slavish renewal of the misguided taste of the day before yesterday'.

The reception rooms upstairs are reached by a back staircase. This means coming directly into the Long Gallery, rather than approaching it through its ante-rooms. A Long Gallery is an anachronism in a house of the 1660s, but a happy one. The ceiling plasterwork is again by Bradbury and Pettifer with the heavy richness of the late 17th century. Scallop shells and palm fronds dance along the frieze. Roman emperors gaze down from medallions. Contemporary family portraits hang along the walls beneath. In sunlight the whole room shimmers white and gold, the rush mats on the floor giving off a pleasant rustic smell.

A small library, the Talbot Room, leads to the Queen's Room. This has an ebullient alabaster mantelpiece that seems to grow in self-importance the closer it approaches the ceiling.

balustrade panels, in painted limewood. Voluptuous scrolls of acanthus toss and tumble down the flights. Baskets of fruit adorn the newel posts. More acanthus, now in plaster, decorates the frieze and seems to drop like ripe fruit from the ceiling. The undersides of the stairs frame paintings by Laguerre.

The stairs are now considered by the National Trust too precious to be used. When will they say this of whole houses? Instead, the downstairs rooms must be visited first and those

Sutton Scarsdale hall

★ Relic of a Smith of Warwick Georgian mansion

At Sutton Scarsdale, 10 miles NW of Matlock; English Heritage, open all year

A good spot for picnics, says the English Heritage handbook. The old Earls of Scarsdale would have agreed. In 1724 they had Francis Smith of Warwick recast their mansion along the bluff from Bolsover and Hardwick. In the 1920s, their successors, the Arkwrights, stripped the house of its contents, three panelled rooms ending up in the Philadelphia Museum of Art. They thought of blowing the place up with dynamite but instead left some of the most exquisite stucco in the North to rain and ruin.

Decades later, with demolition imminent, Sir Osbert Sitwell set out from neighbouring Renishaw to see what he could rescue. The reputed home of the rake in *Rake's Progress*, to Sitwell it embodied the art of the Italian revival in England. Here the *stuccadores*, Artari and Vassalli, brought the sunshine of southern Rococo to the northern uplands. Sitwell found the house already gutted. Four Venetian mantelpieces, 'all of the richest work imaginable, richer by far than anything in a Venetian palace', were still hanging in the air, coloured stucco dripping from their panels. He paid ten shillings and sent workmen and carts to remove them. They found them already fallen and smashed to pieces. But the ruin itself became Sitwell property.

Tended by English Heritage, the house is still a roofless ruin, although no more ruined than Uppark, in West Sussex, after its fire. An imaginative millionaire could research and restore it. Smith's design is robust Baroque, with a fine east façade gazing out over the valley.

The whole structure is in pink stone, now gnarled and weather-beaten with neglect. Inside, scraps of plasterwork, scrolls of gilding, the odd fireplace, cornices and grotesques can be made out. Mostly the walls have been stripped to their brickwork. Sutton Scarsdale is a romantic spot but eerie. It is like an old dowager who has returned from her last ball, thrown aside her clothes and stands suddenly naked.

Tissington hall

★ ★ Jacobean house and estate on the edge of the Peaks

At Tissington, 4 miles N of Ashbourne; private house, open part year

The hall lies in a picturesque enclave reached through park gates on the edge of the Peak District. The green, church, cottages, stables and hall seem all of a piece. The main house lies through a handsome Jacobean gate across a lawn. It is outwardly a rectangular box with none of the usual Jacobean trimmings but with round chimneys dotted along the parapet. It has belonged to FitzHerberts since the 15th century. The family still valiantly maintains both house and estate as a going concern.

The interior is a typically English mixture of styles. The house was built in 1609, symmetrical and with a front-to-back hall as at Hardwick. The porch leads directly into the hall, a low, warm room still with its Jacobean panelling but with 18th-century Gothick decoration. This includes a frieze of delicate ogees and a bold neo-medieval fireplace, all of 1757. The Chippendale dining chairs are also Gothick, as are the far windows, making the room an enjoyable marriage of styles.

The adjacent dining room has a panelled inglenook, possibly remaining from an old kitchen fireplace. Again like Hardwick, Tissington appears to have been planned with service rooms on the ground floor and formal rooms above. Two portraits by Ramsay, of George III and Queen Charlotte, hang over the staircase. Upstairs, the T-shaped East Drawing Room offers a light, airy alcove over the porch. It has the best panelling in the house, pilastered beneath a beautifully restored plaster cornice, and hung with family portraits by Angelica Kauffmann.

The Edwardians added a library to the rear of the house, designed by Arnold Mitchell. It is pleasantly cluttered with old books and maps and has a bold inglenook in the manner of Norman Shaw, who regarded no living room as complete without one. Its frieze depicts an Art Nouveau forest of flora and fauna.

Wingfield manor

★ ☆ Ruin remains of a major medieval palace

Near South Wingfield, 6 miles SE of Matlock; English Heritage, open by arrangement

This was no manor, but a palace. Wingfield must rank as one of England's least-known great ruins. It leaps out of the landscape on its mound above the River Amber, a bristling rampart of 15th-century stonework. Chimneys and gables soar into the sky. The area of its courtyards is larger even than Haddon Hall.

The house was built by Ralph Lord Cromwell, Treasurer to the hapless Henry VI and richest man in England. He began Wingfield as his principal house in the 1440s, shortly after completing Tattershall Castle. The house later passed to the Earl of Shrewsbury and thus fell within the panoply of Bess of Hardwick. It was one of the many prisons of Mary, Queen of Scots. The house was slighted in the Civil War and, although partly restored as a formal house, became mostly a farm, as part of it still is. The ruins are approached along a muddy farm track and the area is heavy with the scent of manure.

The outer courtyard is still flanked by medieval walls, into parts of which the farmhouse has been built. The one complete building to survive, a barn near the entrance, may have been living quarters for servants or visitors. In one corner of the outer court is the High Tower, still climbable and believed to have contained chambers for important guests. The surviving ground floor chamber was a latrine, with evidence of wooden seats over discharge drains. Water cisterns are believed to have flushed them from above, allowing Wingfield to claim the title of first English loo.

Beyond the tower is the inner courtyard. It has the wall of the old guest wing on the left and ahead the customary spread of porch and Great Hall, with kitchens to the left and now vanished solar and family quarters to the right. However, here the pattern is interrupted by a Great Chamber positioned to the left of the screens passage and dividing the Great Hall from the kitchens. This is unusual. The chamber was presumably a reception room for the monarch, there being no room for one at the family end of the Hall. Either way, it is an impressive structure rising to roof height. Its end gable window is like that of a great Perpendicular church.

Although the Great Hall is mostly ruined, its undercroft survives, a magnificent Gothic storeroom with rib vaults of beautifully dressed stone. Wingfield still evokes the grandeur of medieval England. It shows that ruins need not be over-manicured or detached from rural life.

Leighton Hall

shire

Lancashire

'... the most **sensational glazing of any house** in England.'

Astley hall

2 miles W of Chorley; museum, open part year

Astley Hall is the most exhilarating house in Lancashire. I last visited it on a summer afternoon when huge crowds were trooping past to the Royal Lancashire Show in the park. The house was open, free and completely empty. If we cannot promote houses such as these, so admirably rescued from dereliction, they will die a second time.

Astley was the house of the Charnocks of Chorley. Like most of the Lancashire gentry, they were fiercely Catholic in the 16th century and Royalist in the 17th. A Charnock was executed for seeking to dethrone Elizabeth I in the Babington Plot. Their Elizabethan house forms the core of Astley, round an inner courtyard.

In 1653, the last Charnock died without seeing the Restoration, leaving the house to his daughter and her husband, Richard Brooke. In the 1660s, they supplied the front and main reception rooms that we see today. Astley passed by descent, latterly as a preserved 'second seat', through the Brookes, Townley-Parkers and Tattons – all great Lancashire families. It was given to Chorley Council in 1922 as a memorial to the Great War and is well maintained.

The Brooke house is most unusual. It is plainly old-fashioned for its late 17th-century date. Sheets of unadorned windows rise two storeys to a huge long gallery with continuous windows and a parapet. The façade must carry the most sensational glazing of any house in England. The bold functionalism might qualify as 'Modern Movement' neo-Elizabethan. The material is pink stone and brick, now rendered. Two projecting bays flank a wayward classical doorway. Despite first appearances, this composition is not symmetrical, since one side conceals the former medieval hall. The doorway has crudely fashioned paired Ionic columns, crowned by two lions trying to look fierce. The back of the house dates from the earlier building, with a magnificent stepped chimney to the kitchen.

The door opens directly onto the Great Hall. The impact is breathtaking. Astley's hall and parlour have some of the most astonishing plasterwork in England – astonishing rather than beautiful. An apoplectic Pevsner uses the word 'barbaric' three times, as well as 'grim', 'ruthless' and 'breathtaking'. It is as if the young Brookes, loyally Catholic on the outside, decided to order something riotously novel within.

The Great Hall is the chamber of a Renaissance prince. The floor is of rough stone and the bay window is medieval in form, but the walls are lined with panels, divided by pilasters, depicting famous people, a cultured fashion said to predate the Brooke rebuilding. They include Tamerlane and his opponent, Sultan Bajazet; Scanderbeg and his opponent Mohamed II; Columbus and Magellan; Philip II and Leicester; Elizabeth I and Drake; Farnese of Lepanto and Henry IV of France; Spinola (Spanish victor over the Protestant Dutch) and the Hungarian hero, Gabor Bethlen. In other words, the list is carefully chosen to show both sides of each war. The politic Brooke later added the protestant William of Orange.

The walls are overshadowed by the ceiling. This is so enriched with undercut plaster as to defy gravity. Beams are coated with stucco. In each of the panels are wreaths containing cherubs and flowers, carved in three dimensions and some appearing to hang free of the ceiling. The frieze holds shields and cherubs cavorting amid garlands. Much of the craftsmanship is crude and some of the figures are not of plaster but of painted leather and lead. Adding to the magnificence is the staircase placed directly opposite the entrance, with thick acanthus balustrading and newel posts topped with vases of flowers.

Next to the Great Hall and beginning what would have been the family wing of the old house is the drawing room. Here the same plasterers have been at work and here Pevsner's

Above The Great Hall is most noted for its ceiling, decorated with richly modelled plasterwork; the stucco was made from a mixture of horse hair, mud and wine. Some of the figures were actually fashioned from lead or leather which was then painted to resemble stucco.

word 'barbaric' has some application. The roundels are cluttered with incident and the design is never allowed to breathe. The putti are grotesque and ferns appear as the bones of a skeleton. The effect remains sumptuous. Flemish tapestries and walnut and rosewood furniture are the icing on the cake. The Inlaid Room or library and dining room beyond were rebuilt in 1825 but in Jacobean style, re-using old panelling and family portraits.

Back on the other side of the hall is the morning room, benefiting from the left-hand bay of the façade and with further ceiling stuccowork, here more restrained. The room is furnished as a parlour but with a desk and wall safes reflecting its later use as a rent office. A carved relief of two large fish adorn the overmantel.

Upstairs, Astley has strength in depth. The Cromwell bedroom – oddly named given the allegiance of the family – has unusually enriched panelling and a plaster overmantel dating from the 16th-century house. The four-poster carries the Charnock arms. The Stucco Room is more unusual. Decorated a vivid white-and-blue, it has classical pilasters and a ribbed ceiling. By the fire is a priest's hole. In the Oak Room is 'Cromwell's bed', with the most exquisite inlay on the canopy and floral carvings on the headboard.

The top floor is occupied by a Long Gallery, three of its sides completely fenestrated and in a style that must surely predate the 1660s rebuilding. The floor and ceiling undulate gently from one end to the other like the deck of a ship. In the middle is the longest shovelboard table in existence, 23-feet long and with twenty legs.

Borwick hall

★ Elizabethan house built around an older pele tower

At Borwick, 8 miles NW of Lancaster; private house, open by arrangement

The setting of Borwick is vaguely French. Towers and gables peer over a surrounding wall in the centre of the little village rather than across a spreading estate. The pele tower had an Elizabethan house built by the Bindloss family. The building's glory was briefly revived by *The Times*'s music critic, J. A. Fuller-Maitland, who lived there from 1911 to 1938. It then endured decades of humiliating decline until it was rehabilitated as a dwelling in the 1960s. In 1970 it became a hostel and youth activity centre, and is now institutionalized.

The building is an exciting example of that familiar northern form, a pele with Tudor additions. From the garden terrace, the grey-rendered tower rises four storeys. The Great Hall is in the centre with a three-storey porch and the family wing to the left, all of 1595, as dated by the mason, Alixander Brinsmead, at the top of his staircase. He sought to unite these elements in a harmonious façade by adding a row of four pinnacled gables. The house saw a visit from Charles Stuart on his progress south, to be defeated at Worcester in 1651. Sir Robert Bindloss judiciously absented himself from the house for the occasion.

The interior is of little interest, the rich heraldic overmantels having been scattered by dealers across America. The Great Hall (renamed 'baronial') and the staircase retain echoes of more gracious times. One panelled room survives, as does the upstairs library. At the rear is a cluster of old façades, some in pink stone, with buried among them a picturesque 16th-century timber gallery. This was possibly for the use of cloth spinners.

Browsholme hall

★★☆ Medieval moorland house with Jacobean and Wyatt interiors

5 miles NW of Clitheroe; private house, open part year

The Royal Forest of Bowland, once part of the West Riding of Yorkshire, is still wild England. From Clitheroe north to Lancaster are moors and fells over which kings hunted throughout the Middle Ages. Such parks had to be policed and their ancestral keepers became powers in the land. The Parkers of Browsholme, pronounced 'brusom', go back in line to the 13th century. A Thomas Parker bought the freehold of the property in 1603.

The house's most celebrated occupant was Thomas Lister Parker (1779–1858), antiquarian friend of Charles Towneley (see Towneley Hall, page 106) and patron of Turner, Opie and Northcote. He commissioned the fashionable Jeffry Wyatt (later Wyatville) to extend his old house with classical dining and drawing rooms filled with Grand Tour pictures. In the process, he went the way of many owners, overspending and declining into genteel poverty. Forced to sell the house and much of his beloved collection to a relative, he spent his life staying in the houses of friends, struggling to keep up appearances. The house, proudly maintained by the Parkers to this day, is much as Lister Parker left it.

The approach is glorious. The road rises from the Calder Valley towards the moors. The façade appears down a long, bosky vista, disappearing then reappearing close to. It is informal and plain, with a three-storeyed classical frontispiece. One gabled wing is Jacobean, the other is formed by Wyatt's 1807 dining room, with two storeys here replacing three under the same roofline.

The medieval origins of the house and of the Parkers are immediately asserted in the splendid Hall. It is exactly as one might expect of a long-serving constable of these parts. The walls are thick

with antlers, boots, shields, suits of armour and old buckskin coats. Heavy beams loom overhead. Bobbin chairs flank the fireplace. Much of the furniture is pieced together by estate carpenters from ancient fragments. It is a fine muddle, marred only by being too clean.

The library was cut from part of the hall in 1754. It is dedicated to the antiquarianism of Lister Parker, with the rare diagonal panelling brought from Parkhead near Whalley in 1809 and a Towneley family overmantel. The book shelves are not flat against the walls but in low cases jutting into the room and decorated with church bench-ends. The walls display Jacobite relics and two Devis portraits. On either side of the fire are giant tusks, as if the fireplace were a walrus spoiling for an argument.

Beyond the library are Wyatt's two formal rooms built in 1805–8. The style is Soanian, with sweeping arches and Regency plasterwork, although the drawing room has some neo-Jacobean stucco. The walls are crammed with family portraits and Grand Tour scenes, including works by Northcote, Romney and Batoni. The large dining room must have seemed the height of sophistication when approached from the entrance hall. Muddy boots are exchanged for dancing pumps. Parkers gaze down from every side. This was to have been Lister Parker's finest hour.

Behind these front rooms, Browsholme reverts to pre-Wyatt smaller rooms, dark corridors and vignettes. The ante-room has a magnificent Jacobean overmantel, and stained glass recording generations of Parkers and their connections. The stair window is a kaleidoscope of such glass, apparently assembled from all periods.

Upstairs, the Oak Drawing Room has richly carved panelling of c1700 in the style of Grinling Gibbons, with five distinct tiers of entablature. The bedrooms are panelled with different Bowland woods, installed over the centuries by estate carpenters with a skill that defies dating. A magical house.

Burnley: Towneley hall

★★ Family home of eminent antiquarian and collector

1½ miles SE of Burnley; museum, open part year

The house has seen no fewer than nine incarnations. The ancestral home of the Towneleys (or Townleys) since the 14th century today appears grey, Gothic and forbidding. Its exterior is relieved by fine creeper, a glorious scarlet in autumn. Creeper was once the adornment of every English house but is now mostly stripped by conservationists. Inside the house displays one of Lancashire's most magnificent Great Halls, evocative testament to its most celebrated occupant, the Georgian antiquarian, Charles Towneley (1737–1805).

The Towneleys shared recusancy in the 16th century with virtually all other Lancashire landowners. One member of the family had the last head to be spiked on Temple Bar, an unfortunate honour.

Later they settled for rebuilding their ancestral home to display a vast collection of works of art. Zoffany's picture of Charles Towneley and friends surrounded by his 'marbles' in a London town house became the classic depiction of Grand Tour taste. His collection of classical statuary later formed the basis of the British Museum collection. Towneley Hall is now home to Burnley's art gallery, including a large Victorian collection and the Whalley Abbey vestments, made of 14th-century cloth of gold.

The heart of the house is the Great Hall, rebuilt by Richard Towneley, grandfather of Charles, in 1725 in high English Baroque. Fluted pilasters rise to the entablature, white against deep red walls. At either end, baldacchinos in relief frame classical statues. The ceiling plasterwork is by the early Georgian master, Francesco Vassalli, stuccoist to James Gibbs and others. This gloriously assertive chamber, one of the most splendid in the north of England, is too little known.

The left-hand range is of grand reception rooms in high Regency style, designed by Jeffry Wyatt (later Wyatville). The right-hand range survives from the 17th-century house. It includes a small dining room with diagonal panelling (see Browsholme, page 104) and more plasterwork by Vassalli.

The Long Gallery survives on the top floor above the Wyatt rooms. It is a poignant promenade, having lost almost all its frieze of paintings of Lancashire recusants, which the museum is now trying to reassemble. Small bedrooms have been refitted to display 17th-century Lancashire furniture.

Some of Towneley's exterior stonework is of rare 'watershot' masonry. This involves stones being laid on an inward slant, apparently to assist water evaporation

Below left Extravagant plasterwork and stucco in the Great Hall.

Croxteth hall

★★ Elizabethan house with Queen Anne and Edwardian ranges

At Croxteth, 4 miles NE of Liverpool centre; museum, open part year, park open all year

In the 1960s and 70s, the City of Liverpool fled out of town. Planners left the centre empty and blighted, and covered the precious South Lancashire countryside with suburban housing. This soon enveloped the Croxteth Park estate of the Earls of Sefton, the last of whom died in 1972. The house and park were given to the city. Croxteth is now accessible, enjoyable and well displayed, despite a bad fire in 1952 which destroyed many of the 18th-century interiors. One of the rooms has been left undecorated to show the fire damage, an unnecessary conceit.

The hall appears from the park to be of three periods. A Queen Anne range built for the Molyneux family in 1702 looks over a Baroque terrace, a ponderous Edwardian range forms the entrance and Victorian Gothic wing sits at the rear. Part of the original Tudor building can also be

Above The service wing at Croxteth Hall is peopled with a combination of waxwork effigies (the chef) and actors (the kitchen maid) to give a sense of the ceaseless round of activity below stairs in the Edwardian era. The 'servants' use equipment from the era to prepare the sort of food that would have been served 'upstairs'.

seen, with stone-mullioned windows glimpsed above the Hall kitchens.

The Queen Anne façade is one of the finest of its period in Lancashire. A central doorway comprises a broken pediment above paired attached columns; a panel above contains a flamboyant trophy. The eleven-bay front is of red brick with stone dressings, most jolly. The Edwardian entrance range by J. MacVicar Anderson is a joyless reproduction.

The house is laid out round a central courtyard, part of which is Elizabethan, part Queen Anne. The Molyneuxs enjoyed a surge in fortune following a lucrative marriage in 1771. Shrewdly switching from Catholic to Anglican, they were elevated from Viscounts Molyneux to Earls of Sefton. The house was extended in the 1870s, and in 1902 the west range was rebuilt and enlarged to accommodate the gargantuan sporting parties beloved of Seftons.

The Edwardian period is recalled in the museum presentation of the interior. This may have been the house of the mighty Seftons, but it is now in the care of egalitarian Liverpool City Council. Visitors are thus directed past MacVicar Anderson's grandiloquent staircase to begin in the steward's room, servants' hall, kitchens and pantries, as if applying for the job of scullerymaid rather than visiting the family as guests – or even tourists. Downstairs takes precedence over upstairs. That said, these rooms are admirably furnished, with copious use of waxworks and ladies in period costumes. I could not easily tell them apart.

'Upstairs' takes the form of an Edwardian house party, in the manner of Warwick Castle. The use of effigies is excellent, peopling rooms that would be otherwise empty and meaningless. There are ladies at breakfast, children playing cards and gentlemen relaxing in the smoking room. The contrast between the 'two houses' is forceful, and it works.

Gawthorpe hall

★★ Grand Elizabethan mansion restored by Sir Charles Barry

Near Padiham, 3 miles NW of Burnley; National Trust, open part year, garden open all year

The National Trust's only property in rural Lancashire is disappointing. The present house is attributed to the Elizabethan, Robert Smythson, and was the seat of the Shuttleworths, owners of Gawthorpe from the 14th to the 20th centuries. A Shuttleworth named Ughtred is recorded in 1388, another began the present house in 1600. The social reformer, Sir James Kay-Shuttleworth, restored it from near ruin in 1849 with the help of the architect of the Houses of Parliament, Sir Charles Barry.

His descendant, Lord Shuttleworth, gave it to the National Trust in 1972, to be run by Lancashire County Council. A requirement was that the first-floor rooms be a museum displaying the textile collection of Rachel Kay-Shuttleworth – known universally as 'Miss Rachel' – who died in 1967. Architectural interest is thus confined to the exterior and a handful of the rooms. The grounds are gracefully terraced down to the River Calder.

The exterior is undeniably impressive. The house was probably built round a pele, but rather than erecting a hall to one side, the Jacobeans used the tower as a staircase core, the rooms being arranged round it. The result has a powerful, four-square compactness to which Barry was able to add dramatic embellishment, as he did on a grander scale at Highclere, in Hampshire.

Barry rebuilt the stair tower as a strong central feature. The exterior, however, appears to be authentic Smythson, three storeys of mullioned windows with a dramatic outlook to the back over the valley.

Below left Barry's entrance hall at Gawthorpe is divided by a screen, pierced and ornamented like a rood screen of some Gothic church. The panelling was put in place in 1851, shortly before Barry's Houses of Parliament were completed.
Below right The walls of the drawing room are lined with their original panelling, dating from around 1604. The extravagant stucco ceiling was created in 1605 by two plasterers from Yorkshire, Francis and Thomas Gunby.

Inside, one is immediately aware of Barry. The entrance hall is panelled, and has a church-like screen, reminiscent of a corridor in Barry's Palace of Westminster. A frieze is formed of Shuttleworth portraits. Beyond is the dining room which retains its 1605 screen and minstrels' gallery. The two openings beneath were allegedly designed for the performance of plays. The fireplace carries the Kay-Shuttleworth coat of arms and the neo-Jacobean ceiling is a copy of what was there before.

The drawing room, still on the ground floor, is the most successful room in the house. Mostly original, it is richly panelled with arabesque inlay. The plaster frieze of fruit and foliage is interrupted by free-standing plaster figurines while the ceiling is a whirl of geometry and foliage. The room's furniture boasts an octagonal table by A. W. N. Pugin and J. G. Crace, resting on ogival supports. On either side of the fireplace are two huge wooden armchairs, composed from older backs and looking most uncomfortable.

The staircase is by Barry, looking cramped in the confined space left him by Smythson. On the top floor, an old bedroom contains a 1650s bed. Its superb crewel-work Tree of Life was embroidered by Rachel Kay-Shuttleworth copying ancient motifs found throughout the house.

The Long Gallery has a Jacobean ceiling and classical frieze, its character set by Pugin's vivid wallpaper. Portraits are mostly school of Lely but include two splendid Knellers. These were lent by the National Portrait Gallery. Throughout the house are examples of the crewel-work and other embroidery collected by Miss Rachel.

Haigh hall

⭐ A Victorian mansion built in classical style

At Haigh, 2 miles NE of Wigan; museum, open part year

To each Lancashire town its 'hall'. Wigan's Haigh Hall was that of the ancient owners of the town, the Bradshaighs. In 1770, the line died out and the estate overlooking the town was inherited by Elizabeth Dalrymple, who married the 23rd Earl of Crawford and Balcarres. The earl was an enterprising Regency 'improver'. On his marriage, he moved south from Scotland to develop his new-found coal and iron resources of the Wigan area.

In 1827, his son, no less enterprising and an engineer, decided to rebuild the old hall with a dignity more fitting for an earl. He reputedly drew up the plans himself, lived on the site and was his own clerk of works. All the materials were produced in the Wigan area, including the hard sandstone for the walls, the ironwork and the wood. The craftsmanship is superb. The earl laid out 40 miles of walks in the grounds, employing large numbers of local workers during the cotton recession of 1861–3. Haigh Hall passed to Wigan Council in 1947 and was heavily municipalized, with too much signage and tarmac.

The exterior is logical and classical, its chief virtue being the view out over the town from the tiers of bay windows. Behind its severe Tuscan porch, the Entrance Hall has a painting of a fine stag at bay over the fireplace. To the rear and off-centre, a huge staircase fills the heart of the house and is unquestionably its finest feature. It rises to a wide domed lantern resting on sail-vaults, wide billowing arches with decorated lunettes. The plasterwork is said to be Parisian, with eagles and grotesques, griffins and acanthus. It might be a hot-air balloon, ready to rise gracefully into the sky.

Similar plasterwork adorns the main reception rooms, now run together for weddings and other 'events' but which, until 1947, housed the Lindsay Library of the 25th Earl, one of the best collections of books then in private hands. Outside in the park, all Wigan is at play. At the present rate of sprawl, these ancestral estates may yet be the only Lancashire greenery to survive. Haigh is the more precious.

Hall i' th' Wood

⭐⭐ Medieval timber-framed house with 17th-century stone range

2 miles N of Bolton; museum, open all year

This is chocolate-box Elizabethan. The house with the quaint name on the outskirts of Bolton must be reached through a housing estate that shows it no respect at all. There is only an apology for a 'wood', but the glimpse of the house down a short approach is delicious. The exterior includes some of the most exotic black-and-white studding in the county, with overhanging upper floors and cusped St Andrew's crosses.

The original house was built for a clothing family, the Brownlows, who held property here in 1483, but work appears to have stopped with the Great Hall. The domestic wing extended behind rather than across the end. This wing was rebuilt in 1648 by a leading Puritan, Alexander Norris, on the doubtless considerable spoils of confiscating property from the plentiful Lancashire Royalists. He added the two-storeyed entrance porch and the flourish of finials.

The house later became the home and workplace of Samuel Crompton, inventor of the spinning mule in 1779, to whom much of the interior is now dedicated. It then degenerated into tenements and was near derelict when bought, restored and given to the local council by Lord Leverhulme, a Bolton man, in 1899. Many old features were imported and the house is afflicted by museumitis. The only guide is aimed at children. When I arrived, I was greeted with deep suspicion for not having brought a child. Such is the cult of education.

Below The Brownlow bedroom, named after its builders, the Brownlow family, dates from the 1590s. When Lord Leverhulme bought Hall i' th' Wood in 1899 he began buying up suitable pieces of 16th- and 17th-century furniture for the house; the tester bed, made in 1627, originally came from Swinsty Hall in Yorkshire.

Hall i' th' Wood's exterior shows a typical Lancashire marriage of black-and-white on one side and sandstone on the other. It is as if a stern squire had gone to market and returned with a painted lady on his arm. The interior is similarly variegated. The old Great Hall has lost much of its character; the screen has gone, though the wall mortices survive. Behind, in the stone part of the house is the dining room kitted out by Leverhulme with a ceiling copied from a Bolton inn and panelling from Hertfordshire. The overmantel has caryatids with tiny breasts.

Up a fine Restoration staircase is the drawing room, again refurbished by Leverhulme in the style of the 17th-century house. Here, the caryatids' breasts are bigger. In the small study over the porch, with a view over the roofs of Bolton, Samuel Crompton worked on his 'mule', spinning thread at a fraction of the cost of hand-spinning.

The upper rooms are mostly devoted to Crompton's life and work. An artist, musician and inventor, he naturally fell foul of machine-breaking rioters and often had to hide himself and his machine in the attic at Hall i' th' Wood. In one of the rooms, the mule has been rebuilt and set as depicted in a charming portrait of Crompton, sitting by his machine playing a violin. Next door is a small exhibition of the house's benefactor, another local boy made good, William Lever, who rose to become Lord Leverhulme of Port Sunlight.

Heaton hall

✩ ✩ ✩ Magnificent Georgian villa, designed by James Wyatt

Near Prestwich, 4 miles N of Manchester centre; museum, open part year, park open all year

The Heaton Egertons were 16th-century magnates and relatives of the Egertons of Tatton Old Hall (see page 48). The discovery of coal to the north of Manchester in the 18th century brought them huge wealth. In 1772, at the age of twenty-three, Sir Thomas Egerton was able to rebuild the old family home at Heaton with the aid of the already fashionable James Wyatt, who was just twenty-six. They produced the most handsome house of its period in Lancashire, and Wyatt's finest surviving house anywhere. Egerton became Earl of Wilton but died without male heirs. The house passed to a younger line of the Grosvenor family and was sold to Manchester Corporation, minus its principal furniture and art, in 1901. The city was acquiring much needed open space. The Corporation thought the house might be useful as a tea-room, nothing more.

Although valiant efforts have been made to restore some contents and dignity to Heaton, a century of municipal ownership has drained the house of humanity. Worse, the conservationists have

Above On the first floor of Heaton Hall is the Cupola Room. Wyatt's rotunda was inspired by the architecture of Robert Adam and the painted decoration is by Biagio Rebecca, an Italian-born artist who made his career in Britain. His speciality was painting that imitated classical bas-relief sculpture. Rebecca collaborated with Robert Adam on several buildings, including Kedleston Hall (see page 86).

drawn all the blinds. From the outside, the house looks closed even when it is open and from the inside it looks as if someone has just died. The point of Heaton's location was to look out over the Manchester skyline. On my last visit, the house seemed under a shroud.

The south front is one of Wyatt's most serene works, every bit a match for the façades of his contemporary, Robert Adam. The house is just two storeys high, a villa rather than a mansion. A three-bayed central bow is flanked by Venetian windows with, on each side, a colonnade and two pavilions also with Venetian windows.

The composition has both balance and symmetry. The entrance, to the rear, leads into a hall and staircase but these rooms are wholly subordinate to the main enfilade on the south side. In the middle is the saloon, Wyatt classicism fortissimo. The room is painted in soft blues and greens, with a frieze of harps by Joseph Rose, Adam's stuccoist. It has been filled with Wyatt furniture removed by the government from his other great interior, Heveningham Hall in Suffolk, when that was being sold to a private owner.

To one side of the saloon is the dining room, with an exquisite apsidal alcove decorated with Bacchanalian medallions. The chairs here are also from Heveningham. On the other side, the billiard

Above Biagio Rebecca's skills as a painter of antique motifs were put to good use in the music room where he painted the grisaille panels that decorate the organ. The chamber organ was made by Samuel Green, the leading organ maker of his day. One of Green's patrons was George III and in 1789 Green had completed an instrument for St George's Chapel at Windsor Castle, commissioned by the king.

room has pride of the place, the table by Gillow being one of the first installed in an English house. The room has kept its historical wall paintings, grand classical scenes by a Polish artist, Michael Novosielski, said to be his only surviving works.

Lord Wilton was an enthusiastic cellist who inaugurated the music room at Heaton with a grand concert of works by Handel and Corelli in August 1789. The following year, a Samuel Green organ was installed, with Rococo panels painted in grisaille. The ceiling looks naked and was surely meant to be painted. Beyond is the library with bookcases by Gillow.

The staircase is Wyatt at his most grandiose. Shallow flights rise to a pillared landing running round three sides of the hall and lit by a magnificent Venetian window. Here is the finest room in the house, the Cupola Room, which is in the Etruscan style normally associated with Adam. This is one of Wyatt's few such imitations. The delicate paintings in the pilasters and ceiling panels are by Biagio Rebecca. It is a lovely room, comparable with Adam's Etruscan Room at Osterley Park, in west London. But, at least during opening hours, it should be allowed the light of day.

Hoghton tower

Near Hoghton, 5 miles SW of Blackburn; private house, open part year

The view of Hoghton painted in 1736 by Arthur Devis is one of the finest country house pictures. It shows the house exposed on a naked hill at the end of a long rising avenue, the Lancashire plain spread round it on all sides. The hill is now encased in woodland, but it is still possible on a clear day to see the Lake District and Snowdonia from the heights of Hoghton.

The estate straddling the Ribble Valley has been in the same line since the 13th century, and once totalled 40,000 acres. Albeit smaller, it is still owned by Sir Bernard de Hoghton. In the 1560s, Thomas Hoghton built himself a new house, possibly based on an old keep, round two courtyards. His intention must have been part ostentation, part defence. He was a passionate Catholic and friend of the Jesuit Edmund Campion, eventually going into voluntary exile to Antwerp to escape Elizabethan persecution.

The Hoghtons supported all sides and none in the political turmoil of the 17th and 18th centuries. The house welcomed James I with a massive feast in 1617, its menu proudly preserved. It was here he was said to have knighted a favoured loin of beef, thus inventing 'sirloin'. Later Hoghtons married Nonconformists and defended Lancashire against the Jacobites. The family moved to Preston and the tower on the hill was abandoned to tenants, weavers and gamekeepers. Not until the antiquarian, Sir Henry Hoghton, inherited the estate in 1862 was the old seat restored. He added a medieval 'de' in his surname and employed Paley & Austin to re-create a suitably antique place. Most of the interiors are from this time.

Above The Great Hall at Hoghton is known as the banqueting hall; it was here that James I and his retinue feasted and here that the king knighted the joint of beef 'Sir Loin'. Among other dishes enjoyed at the banquet in August 1617 were roast swan, cold roast heron, boiled chickens, venison pasties, turkey pie, curlew pie and dried hogs' cheeks.

Hoghton Tower appears well fortified from the approach up nearly a mile of avenue. The central stone gatehouse is flanked by walls and battlemented towers, leading to the first of two courtyards on the slope. Both are original to the 16th-century house, the lower one surrounded by offices and much restored. Fine iron gates lead to a second gate-tower behind which is a higher courtyard. This formed the heart of the 16th-century house.

The Great Hall is unusually on the left of the court, suggesting an earlier keep to which it might have been attached. It is at the top of an enticing flight of steps and has two tall bay windows at the dais end. The one on the far side looks out over the steepest part of the hill. With the kitchens and offices in the outer court, family rooms could extend comfortably round the inner one. They form a remarkable sequence. Those downstairs are mostly Elizabethan or Jacobean, used by the family and for business.

They include the Guinea Room, decorated with coins symbolizing the estate rents. In this room, it was said, a Hoghton baronet gambled away the entire site of the city of Liverpool.

Upstairs are the state rooms, celebrating the royal visit of 1617. The Buckingham Room honours James's constant companion, the Duke of Buckingham. The state bedroom houses a magnificent Elizabethan bed with intricate carved panels. The ballroom contains a severe classical fireplace and an eccentric Mannerist one. All the panelling is by Gillow, as are the quite exceptional superb neo-Georgian doorways.

Across the King's Staircase is the suite in which James I himself stayed. The rooms are ancient and intimate, their windows surveying the surrounding landscape as they would have done four centuries ago. The king remained here for only two days. The cost brought the Hoghtons close to ruin. They are at last able to claim some return.

Ince Blundell hall

★ ★ Early Georgian house with Pantheon gallery

At Ince Blundell, 4 miles S of Southport; private house, open by arrangement

Those who would visit the great recusant house of Ince Blundell must brave the Canonesses of St Augustine, Nursing Sisters of the Mercy of Jesus. Their purchase of the great house of the Blundells in 1960 was, according to the Mother Superior at the time, in every sense 'an act of faith'. The act has been admirably honoured both as a religious convalescent home and as a work of architectural conservation.

The Blundells arrived at Ince in the 13th century. They were later linked by marriage to many of the great recusant families, to Tempests, Stonors and Welds. Robert Blundell began the present house, designed by the Liverpool architect, Henry Sephton, in about 1720. Blundell's son, Henry, an antiquarian with the same obsessive taste as Charles Towneley (see Towneley Hall, page 106), gave the hall its present character. He first built a Doric temple in the garden for his sculptures. When this was outgrown in 1802, Blundell added a large Pantheon on the far side of the garden front.

The interior of the Pantheon is covered in ornamental coffering. It is heartbreaking to see photographs of it before the sale of its statues to Liverpool's Walker Gallery in 1960. These surely could be returned to help re-found what had been one of the most important Grand Tour galleries in the country.

Left The drawing room at Ince Blundell Hall, now furnished with a dining table and chairs, was decorated in the mid-18th century. The wall panels are painted with classically inspired motifs, much in the manner of Robert Adam. **Below** Attached to the Hall is a chapel, now the Catholic parish church of the Holy Family. Built in 1858 it was the work of Roman Catholic architect, J. J. Scoles, designer of several Victorian Catholic churches including the Farm Street church in Mayfair.

In 1837 the house passed to Thomas Weld of Lulworth Castle in Dorset, on condition that he changed his name to Blundell. In 1847 he commissioned J. G. Crace to redecorate the dining room and picture gallery. The result is outstanding, quite unlike the rich Italianate interiors that Crace produced for Longleat, in Wiltshire, or Knightshayes, in Devon.

The wall panels of the drawing room carry delicate painted grotesques, a light-hearted Adamish design of *c*1750. Bunches of grapes drip from the ceiling. The smaller music room next door has a Rococo ceiling containing an eagle and gold thunderbolts. The dining room is by Crace, but the walls are embarrassingly filled with blown-up Italian photographs of woodland scenes, replacing the tapestries moved by the Welds to Lulworth. There they can be seen today in the new house, splendid but sadly removed in spirit.

The chapel walls are by Crace, with delicate Italian motifs surrounding large grisaille panels. This is now the local Catholic parish church. Meanwhile the old sitting room has been converted by the Sisters into their private chapel. It is one of the most endearing rooms in the house and also has walls by Crace. Ince Blundell may have lost its works of art, but it remains a monument to the talents of this underrated craftsman.

LANCASTER Cottage museum

★ Tiny cottage opposite Lancaster castle

Castle Hill, Lancaster; museum, open part year

In 1961, the buildings facing the castle's entrance were declared unfit for human habitation. In the manner of the age, they were to be demolished. By a miracle they escaped and are now a town treasure. Nos. 15 and 17 were once a single house with the date 1739 over the door, although the interiors look older. The windows once had stone mullions. In the 19th century, the property was cut in two: half is now a private house and the other half is open to the public.

The cottage is one of the smallest I know. It consists of a single parlour downstairs with a scullery and wash-house at the back, and two tiny, sparsely-furnished bedrooms upstairs. In the parlour the family lived, fed and spun, as did most out-workers in cloth-rich Lancaster. The fireplace is still open. There are boxes to keep salt, candles and knives free from damp. On the floor are rag rugs.

The small wash-house has a stove/boiler and a cellar beneath. There is no well or privy. Both were in the garden and have long vanished. All the place needs is more junk and dirt and an aspect onto what should be the busy heart of the town.

LANCASTER
Judges' lodgings

⋆⋆ Late 17th-century town house with Gillow furniture

Church Street, Lancaster; museum, open part year

The house is located at the top of a flight of steps looking down Church Street. The castle is its backdrop, with the original Gillow furniture works to the left. The view to the other end of Church Street is of Pevsner's 'grandest monument in England', the Ashton Memorial on the distant hillside outside the town. It was designed by John Belcher in 1906, the last age to dare such follies in the landscape.

The house façade has the rough-and-tumble classicism of the 1670s. Seven bays of soft ochre stone rise above a jolly doorway with a colourful pediment. Its panel contains a coat of arms and the red rose of Lancaster. The house is no longer judges' lodgings and is used as a museum. Inside is an earlier entrance hall decorated with pikes, muskets and a set of stocks. On the walls are portraits, some by George Romney, of distinguished Lancaster merchants, most of them slave-traders. Off the hall is the old parlour, containing a superb desk of 1778.

The main reception rooms are upstairs and house a superb exhibition of Gillow furniture. The splendour of these rooms shows that the Court's visit was an important social event. Drawing room and dining room are beautifully furnished and enjoy views down Church Street. Opposite is an early billiard room, Gillow being the first extensive manufacturer of such tables.

The senior or 'hanging' judge's bedroom displays the wig, gown and even the black cap for passing the death sentence. The furniture is appropriately lugubrious, including a large wardrobe in Gillow's Regency style. In the massive bed, the judge slept alone (we assume) with his conscience. On the staircase is a cruel caricature of John Wesley preaching in Rochdale and other prints of legal and political Lancashire.

Lancaster is a sad place, the denuded capital of a lost dukedom. The town is splendidly set on a hill but has been besieged by pylons and industrial sprawl. At its heart is not a busy market or great cathedral but, of all things, a Victorian prison still in use. In the 1960s, a disastrous decision located the new Lancaster University not in the town, which it might have regenerated, but on green-belt land outside it.

Nonetheless, an enclave of old streets and buildings survives immediately beneath the castle. These are overseen by the residence of the castle's Keeper, later the lodgings of the Circuit judges. From here, Keeper Thomas Covell hunted down the ten 'Pendle Witches' in 1612.

Right The centrepiece of the dining room is a Gillow table, made in 1822, the year that Richard Gillow bought Leighton Hall. The furniture maker was founded in around 1730 by Robert Gillow, Richard's grandfather.

Leighton hall

★ ★   Gothick house with Gillow furniture and Lakeland views

At Yealand Conyers, 9 miles N of Lancaster; private house, open part year

The site is the finest in Lancashire, a platform in the midst of a sweeping park with the crags of Silverdale and the Lake District beyond. Although the house exterior is of no great distinction, it contrives to take on the grandeur of its surroundings.

Leighton passed through many hands until rebuilt in 1763 for the Towneleys of Towneley Hall (see page 106), whose zest for property knew no bounds. In 1822, the house was sold to Richard Gillow of the Lancaster furniture firm and has remained in the same family ever since, housing a superb collection of Gillow furniture. The exterior and hall were gothicized in the 1820s, and in 1870 a three-storey billiard room wing was added by Paley & Austin. This wing now dominates the main front, rather spoiling its symmetry.

The entrance hall and staircase are Gothick and enjoyably cluttered with trophies, hats and sporting prints. Three slender arches screen an elegant staircase. Doorways all have pointed arches. The adjacent dining room is the star of the house. It has Gillow dining chairs of a sinuous solidity, offset by a massive Jacobean carver at one end. The ceiling plasterwork is an unusual lierne pattern, its central oval originally intended to light that essential of every Gillow house, a billiard table. The walls carry French pastoral paintings fixed to the panelling. The spectacular portrait of Mrs Reynolds, mother of the present owner, is by Edward Seago.

The other rooms are those of a comfortable Regency house, occupied by a family manifestly of the Catholic faith. The library leads into the drawing room, with superb views to the Lakes beyond. The furniture is various in style, Gillows being 'catholic' in taste as well as religion. A lady's workbox combines as a desk with niches for Catholic figurines. The house has an excellent collection of English landscape and genre paintings, including a Jordaens and a fine Morland. Upstairs is a tiny recusant chapel.

The music room in the Victorian wing saw the last private recital by the contralto, Kathleen Ferrier. It contains a fine picture of St Jerome, once thought to be by Domenichino. The gardens are arranged to take advantage of the site. Leighton also has a reputedly ferocious collection of birds of prey.

LIVERPOOL

Lennon house

★ Suburban home of late pop legend

Mendips, Menlove Avenue, Woolton, Liverpool;
National Trust, open part year for guided tours only

Right When the National Trust took on Mendips the decor had changed considerably in the 40 years since Lennon lived there and no record survived of how the rooms might have looked. The Trust decided to furnish Lennon's bedroom as if it were the late 1950s, when John went to art school to study lettering and started his first band; pop posters are tacked up on the wall and a draughtsman's T-square stands at the foot of the bed.

Not content with Forthlin Road (right), the National Trust acquired in 2002 another extremely modest work of 20th-century Liverpool architecture. It is the three-bedroom semi-detached house to which the five-year-old John Lennon moved in 1945. He was brought up there by his Aunt Mimi after his parents separated, and his mother was killed by a bus in the road outside. It was in a bedroom here that the introverted youth dreamed his musical future. On the front porch he played his guitar when his aunt and her other lodgers, mostly veterinary students, could stand it no more inside.

The house was donated to the National Trust by Lennon's widow, Yoko Ono, when she heard it was to become a 'Beatles themed hotel'. She told the Trust, 'He was always in his room, thinking, dreaming – he was an incredible dreamer. I particularly wanted to save his bedroom, instead of their ruining it by making it a honeymoon suite ... Once I walked in there, it was like walking into that childhood.'

The house is considerably more genteel than the McCartney house. Situated on a dual carriageway in Woolton, it has the rendered exterior, canted windows and hipped roof of tens of thousands of inter-war houses of the New Ideal Homes movement. There is a garden front and back.

The interior has been restored by the Trust in the ascetic style of the 1950s. There is a touch of Arts and Crafts in the staircase window and a touch of Art Deco in the tiled fireplaces and mirrors, but both attributions are stretching a point. Lennon's own room has been evocatively re-created. It has Bardot and Presley posters, 45 rpm records by Lonnie Donnegan and Little Richard, and coffee mugs.

Everywhere are reminders of Aunt Mimi's famous warning: 'The guitar's all very well, John, but you'll never make a living at it.'

McCartney house

⭐ Council-home of young Paul McCartney

20 Forthlin Road, Allerton, Liverpool; National Trust, open part year for guided tours only

This is where Paul McCartney lived as a boy and where he and Lennon wrote their early songs. As McCartney writes in the guidebook: 'My Mum and Dad would have found it hard to believe that the house is now a National Trust property – you expect the National Trust to own places like Blenheim Palace, not a little terrace house like this. But they would be chuffed.' We might share their bafflement.

Apart from assiduous rubber-neckers with a good map, the house is accessible only to National Trust coach parties. The 1950s estate house, off suburban Mather Avenue, was taken by the McCartneys in 1955 when Paul was thirteen. Designed by the City Architect, Sir Lancelot Keay, it was called 'Intermediate Type Standard Building 5'. Of two storeys, the exterior had a simple two-bay façade with Georgian-style sashes.

Above When the National Trust came to re-create the 1950s interiors at Forthlin Road they were able to use contemporary photographs taken by Mike McCartney as a guide. Pictures show Paul McCartney and John Lennon rehearsing and composing songs in front of the living-room fire; Paul's father Jim, an amateur musician, was presumably more tolerant of their early attempts than John's aunt Mimi and her lodgers.

Is this now a style? Inside are a hall, sitting room, dining room and kitchen downstairs and three bedrooms upstairs. The roof slopes. In front is a small area surrounded by a privet hedge. To the back is a tiny garden with shed and outside WC, although there was also one upstairs. The family had a television by 1953. This was unquestionably smarter housing than would have been available at the time for working-class families living in central Liverpool. Owned by the council, it cost £1,369.9s.1d to build.

Paul's mother died in 1956 but it was from here that he met George Harrison on the bus to school and John Lennon at a Woolton fete. They formed a band in 1958. By 1963 they were already history and the Forthlin Road house was uninhabitable for the crowds outside. In July the following year, Paul bought his father a large house in Heswall on the Dee estuary, moving him out at dead of night to avoid publicity. With no respect for history, his aunts recklessly painted over the Beatles' doodled lyrics on the toilet wall. Perhaps, like medieval frescoes, they can be recovered. A later occupant, Mrs Jones, gave visiting fans snippets of the old lace curtains as mementos.

The house was bought by the National Trust in 1995. Some Fifties furniture was acquired and a selection of photos of the band by Mike McCartney, Paul's photographer brother, put on display.

Sudley hall

⭐ Ship-owner's house with fine art collection

Mossley Hill, Aigburth, Liverpool; museum, open part year

The house is typical of dozens of mansions built by Liverpool shipping magnates on the slopes of Sefton Park and Mossley Hill in the mid-19th century. Visitors to Liverpool must pinch themselves to appreciate that this was once the greatest concentration of conspicuous wealth in Britain, if not the world. The Holt family built solidly and collected prodigiously. George Holt's gallery of mostly English 18th- and 19th-century works was left to the city on his daughter's death in 1944.

The house exterior is exceptionally severe, Grecian revival of *c*1830. A Doric porch is flanked by walls of Lancashire 'new red sandstone', free of decoration and relieved on the garden side only by a small conservatory. The interior is a contrast, warm and rich, dating mostly from the 1880s. It houses the Holt collection in all its glory.

The rooms are similar in their present decoration, mostly panelled and with stencilled or hand-blocked wallpaper. They are sparsely furnished but with Pre-Raphaelite tiled fireplaces. In the library is Millais' *Vanessa*. The Drawing Room contains a fine Gainsborough of Lady Folkestone, a Romney, a Raeburn and a Reynolds. In the dining room are Turner's *Rosenau Castle* and a large Landseer of a Scottish hunting party. The Morning Room is devoted to the Pre-Raphaelites, pride of place going to Holman Hunt's *Finding of the Saviour in the Temple*, and a Leighton of a girl reading a book. The house guide was written by the late George Melly, who used to visit Sudley Hall as a child.

Lytham hall

⭐⭐ Carr of York house of 1750s

Near Lytham, 6 miles SE of Blackpool; private house, open by arrangement

At first sight, Lytham might be a Georgian mansion in the Home Counties. Set in flat parkland near the centre of Lytham St Annes, its redbrick-and-white dressings are unusual in sandstone Lancashire. Perhaps the seaside was considered no place for stone. Or as Sacheverell Sitwell said of its creator, Carr of York, 'His buildings could stand as well in any part of England.'

As recently as the 1960s, Lytham was still owned and occupied by the Clifton family, one of the oldest landowners in the county. Their estate of 16,000 acres embraced Lytham and much of the Fylde up to Blackpool. Staunchly Catholic, they endured a terrible 17th century, four sons dying in the Civil War. Yet the family recovered sufficiently after the Restoration to pull down the old house and, in 1757, commission a new one from Carr of York.

The Cliftons' interest in the estate collapsed in the 20th century. Land was sold, the house contents dispersed and the building passed to Guardian Assurance in 1963. The company did it proud, with the possible exception of its sense of colour. The house was restored and has now passed to a local trust, which is struggling to reassemble pictures, furniture and mementos of the Clifton past.

The house is magnificent to its drive, three storeys with a rusticated ground floor and a central pediment above Ionic pilasters. The plan is conventional, the decoration not. The entrance hall has

Above The entrance at Lytham opens into a wide hall, decorated with restrained plasterwork. The more florid examples of stucco are placed above doorways and framed wall panels. The door into the staircase hall is set in an arch; the doorway, in turn, is framed by two columns, topped by an open-bed pediment.

pedimented doorcases and a low-relief stucco ceiling, the roundel a swirling Rococo work. Similar stucco is found in the adjacent morning room and dining room, the latter with a wide apse in a tentative Adam style. However, by the time the ballroom was built, Adam's neo-classicism is firmly in the ascendant.

The staircase hall at the rear of the building is one of Carr's finest works. The flights rise, divide and return to a landing. Here the lower door from the hall is answered in a Venetian screen, behind which Carr created a Baroque inner door. The order is Ionic below, Corinthian above. The whole composition is most satisfying. Nor is that all. The ceiling is a tremendous decorative flourish. The Rococo roundel contains a relief of Jupiter, decorated with facial make-up and a red staff. It looks as if medical students have been at work after a party.

In a house of fine craftsmanship little altered since it was built, the carved chimneypieces in the bedrooms take the palm. The house is filled with works collected by the trust and not yet distributed to the rooms. On a back stair I encountered a huge Gustave Doré. Near a side entrance is a Richard Westall of Cardinal Wolsey. Some rooms are now panelled and furnished. Lytham is fighting its way back to life.

Martholme

⭐ Remaining fragment of a medieval hall house

Near Great Harwood, 5 miles N of Blackburn; private house, open by arrangement

Martholme is chiefly of archaeological interest. Thousands of such houses must have survived into the 19th century, only to fall down or be wiped out by careless owners. Martholme is at the end of a quiet lane beneath a magnificent railway viaduct. It is an attractive grouping of medieval gatehouse and fragment of a hall house, apparently its service wing and screens passage. The rest of the hall has vanished but the wing has been joined by a passage to a detached timber-framed kitchen, later encased in stone.

The original house belonged to the lords of the Heskeths from 1289. The Hesketh double-headed eagle is carved into a wall. The rest of the old house is believed to have collapsed in the 17th century. The remnants were tenanted and finally sold in 1819. The building is now occupied by the Codling family, who love it dearly.

Of the original interiors, only the former buttery and pantry survive. In one wall is set a strangely wide doorway leading to what must once have been an outside passage. This looks very 'vernacular'. Across the passage is the former kitchen. In the room above the buttery is a small Gothic window, possibly of the 14th century. Could this have been a secret chapel? Martholme should keep 'house detectives' occupied for hours.

Meols hall

★ ☆ Neo-Georgian manor house built in the 1960s

At Churchtown, 2 miles NE of Southport; private house, open part year

Churchtown's chief claim to fame is to have seen the first potato planted in England (from Ireland), before Raleigh's more celebrated imports from America. The property of the Catholic Heskeths once commanded much of this part of Lancashire, with the recusant Scarisbricks next door. A Hesketh was imprisoned for supporting a Jacobite rising in 1692 and there was reputedly a priest's hole in the house. It later became a farm.

Meols was comprehensively rebuilt by the late Roger Hesketh, who from 1959 began to reassemble the village and surrounding estate after disastrous property sales by his disagreeable father. He created the house to display the family's large collection of paintings. It now clings to the past amid the suburbs of Southport, Torquay of the North.

The house shines like a beacon from the 1960s in sharp contrast to the architectural dreariness of the era. The idea of the Neo-Georgian Hesketh was that the main front in Smith-of-Warwick manner should preside over the fragment of the old Meols Hall, with the service wing 'later Georgian' and the library extension 'Regency'. It was designed to the last detail by Hesketh himself. He even wrote music in the style of Haydn for Churchtown church. His passion for the patrician traditions of old Lancashire were strongly expressed in his building.

The interior of Meols (pronounced Meels) shown to the public is essentially a gallery of paintings and not much else. Yet the effect of wandering through small rooms of dusky pictures and family paraphernalia is strangely reassuring in this bleak corner of Lancashire.

The paintings are mostly family portraits but include a satisfying scatter of landscapes and devotional works. In the library is a superb James Ward of a gigantic white horse. Heskeths and related Bolds rub shoulders with French landscapes and a Brueghel of the *Sermon on the Mount*. There are prints of hare coursing on Formby Sands.

'...a beacon from the 1960s...'

Rufford old hall

★★★ 'Magpie' house with extraordinary movable screen in the Great Hall

At Rufford, 7 miles N of Skelmersdale; National Trust, open part year

Rufford stands with Speke as a champion of Lancashire black-and-white. Its Great Hall is exhilarating and all later additions have deferred to it. The original house was built by the Hesketh family in the early 16th century, highpoint of English timber-framing. It would have been on an H-plan, with wings on either side of the hall. One wing has gone, making way for a pleasant enclosed garden. The other has been replaced by 17th-century and later buildings. The family moved into a neighbouring 'modern' house in the 18th century, but restored it in the 1820s when 'the olden times' came back into fashion. Such is taste. The Heskeths later inherited Easton Neston in Northamptonshire and in 1936 gave Rufford to the National Trust.

The approach to the house is dominated by the exterior of the Great Hall ahead. Part of this is a Victorian reconstruction, including the lantern and left-hand gabled wing, giving the outside too much the appearance of a Swiss chalet (compare Turton Tower, page 148). To the left and at right angles is a redbrick wing of 1662, probably built by a lessee of part of the property. It is handsome and gabled but clearly not modern enough for the Georgian Heskeths. Behind and facing the gardens are façades of all periods, mostly Victorian.

'... crenellated hammerbeams, enriched with angels.'

The interior is essentially the Great Hall. The roof is of crenellated hammerbeams, enriched with angels. At the family end, the wall is coved with a gable filled with black-and-white quatrefoils above and a generous bay window to one side. Every detail is lavishly carved. The doors in the end wall would have led to private apartments, now vanished.

The other end of the hall is even more extraordinary. There is no screens passage as such, instead the wall of the former service wing, decorated with giant quatrefoils and with arches below. The latter have arches enriched with heraldry and Gothic patterns.

In front of this end stands a movable screen, the only such work to survive in England. It is of astonishing decorative force. The panels are filled with Hesketh heraldry and Gothic vine leaves. Above rise three fantastic finials, higher than the body of the screen. I have seen this work, of *c*1530, called barbaric, outlandish, 'medieval Baroque' and even Polynesian. It is certainly the product of a most fertile imagination, showing a decorative freedom soon to be disciplined, some might say crushed, by the Renaissance. This wonderful room embodies the splendour of Lancashire's late Middle Ages.

After this, Rufford is something of an anticlimax, although it has been well presented by the National Trust. The dining room is an 18th-century addition hung with earlier Brussels tapestries. The study, created in the 1830s, is in Jacobean style with an overmantel banged together from old fragments, and tapestries on the walls. The upstairs rooms are Victorian in decoration, enjoyably cluttered.

Above In the Great Hall, the hammerbeams that support the roof braces are decorated with winged angels, carved from wood. Each one bears a shield, once painted with a coat of arms as part of a public show of family heraldry. Arms and crests displayed throughout the Great Hall, some of which still survive, were intended to demonstrate the ancestry of both the Heskeths and their patrons, the Earls of Derby.

Salford: Ordsall hall

★ ☆ House with surviving 15th-century Great Hall

Ordsall Lane, Salford; museum, open all year

Poor Ordsall. One of the great timbered houses of Lancashire once lay on the fertile banks of the River Irwell, a miraculous survival against all odds. It now languishes on a side road near Salford Quays, its wretched garden enfolded in municipal housing and warehouses. It was once a home of the Radclyffes, passing through many hands before being rented by a Pre-Raphaelite painter, F. J. Shields, and then restored by the Egertons of Tatton in the 1880s. Salford Council bought the house in 1959. I hazard the suggestion, but surely the whole building might be moved from this hopeless place to greater dignity on the adjacent Salford Quays.

The house has a Victorian brick exterior to Ordsall Lane and 17th-century extensions. The one important feature is the 15th-century Hall. Outside, it has the dazzling quatrefoil studding found (probably copied) later at Samlesbury. There are not one but two window bays, both generously glazed and jutting out into the former courtyard. With their upper windows and bold gables, they are almost houses in themselves. Such lavish timbering was always a sign of a prosperous owner.

The hall's interior is sensational. It is open to the roof, with quatrefoil panels and trusses everywhere. Most extraordinary is the screen. This is not the customary, horizontal feature with minstrels' gallery but a wall of panelling with a central arch and decorative gable above it, a design more appropriate to a church chancel. The uprights are beautifully moulded and the quatrefoils on the walls have an almost jazzy effect.

At the family end, a bedroom survives with a star-patterned ceiling and simple furniture. But a huge effort of imagination is needed to recapture the aura of this house, once surrounded by fields and simple cottages over which these great windows would have glowed with wealth and welcome.

Samlesbury hall

⭐ ⭐   Hall house with quatrefoil and herringbone timbering

At Samlesbury, 4 miles W of Blackburn; museum, open all year

The seat of the Southworth family is but a fragment of its old self, but this fragment includes a dazzling display of black-and-white architecture. Samlesbury speaks broad Lancastrian. Southworths fought at Agincourt but fell foul of the Reformation and, like many Lancashire families, kept on falling. They were ruined by the 17th century, but at least collected a saint along the way. Father John Southworth was the last Englishman to be executed for his faith, at Tyburn in 1654. His remains are in Westminster Cathedral.

The hall was tenanted until the 19th century when it was partly demolished and became an inn then a girls' school. In 1924 it was about to be demolished and shipped to America, where these buildings are better appreciated, when a group of enthusiasts saved it.

The original hall was three-sided, with a Great Hall and wings. Only the Great Hall and one wing remain, coated in the most vivid black-and-white – herringbone on the 15th-century hall and thick quatrefoil on the left-hand wing. The hall bay has a delightfully romantic gabled chamber jutting above it. Although heavily restored in 1835 and again in the 1860s, the composition is picturesque. The side wing has a rear brick wall with large chimneys, said to be the oldest brick in Lancashire.

The Great Hall's interior is open to the roof, with boldly cusped wind-braces. A huge fireplace dominates one side and a bold bay window the other. The hall used to have a rare free-standing screen, usefully dated 1532, like that at Rufford, but this was dismantled and incorporated into the minstrels' gallery in the 19th century.

The restored parlour is thick with carved panels and ceiling beams. Over the doors are reliefs of Henry VIII and Catherine of Aragon, while two giant coats of arms adorn the overmantel. The entrance hall beyond is a Victorian insertion to link the hall range with the chapel at the end of the wing. This was originally built in 1420, and has Perpendicular windows and a family pew in a gallery.

Upstairs is Samlesbury's Long Gallery. The decorated oak ceiling is of 1545. The rooms are here filled with antiques for sale. They at least appear to have been chosen with some care for the period of the rooms. I would rather have this than that the house be left empty.

Scarisbrick hall

✦✦ Victorian Gothic pile and Pugin-family masterpiece

At Scarisbrick, 4½ miles SE of Southport; private house, open by arrangement

I cannot omit Scarisbrick although, at the time of writing, its owner, Kingswood College, rarely makes it accessible. It can be seen from afar and may be discreetly perambulated with glimpses through the windows to its stupendous interiors. This is one of England's great houses. Threatened with demolition in 1962, the years have surely won it the right to greater display.

Victorian houses usually had a more exciting birth than Georgian ones. Scarisbrick (pronounced Scasebrick) was the product of a marriage of minds between an eccentric and reclusive landowner and a twenty-five-year-old prodigy, Augustus Welby Northcote Pugin. Charles Scarisbrick's family had lived on this land since the Middle Ages. A devout Catholic, he never married but had a mistress and illegitimate family of thirty years' standing. A miser and magpie, he amassed a huge collection of antiquities from all over Europe, leaving a fortune of £3m on his death. None of it was to go to his legal heir, his sister, whom he hated so much that he ordered his death to be kept secret. She fought for and won her rights.

In 1837, Scarisbrick asked Pugin to redesign his much-altered family house on the marshland north of Liverpool. The country, as Humphry Repton had said, 'was too flat and bleak to be deemed picturesque'. What was true in 1802 is more so today. Pugin was working on a building that the Gothic scholar, Thomas Rickman, had already begun, including the new Great Hall. But work proceeded slowly and Pugin was constantly complaining of delay. Scarisbrick took to living in total seclusion, not even talking to his steward. By 1860, Pugin and Scarisbrick were both dead and the house unfinished.

The sister, Anne Scarisbrick, took matters impressively in hand. She hired Pugin's son,

'... the grim, fantastic tower rises over the trees, ...'

Right When A. W. N. Pugin began work at Scarisbrick Hall in 1837 he had designed only one domestic building, his own home, St Marie's Grange. He had worked as a theatrical designer, an experience that may have been useful when creating Gothic-inspired interiors within the existing shell of Thomas Rickman's building. The King's Room is lined with prefabricated panels, carved in imitation of medieval designs and decorated with Tudor-style painted portraits.

the impetuous Edward Welby Pugin, to complete the house with a new wing and the present tower. How far the result is as the elder Pugin intended is a matter of debate. Either way, the house was finished and furnished, and gloriously so. Despite years of abuse and the stripping of most of its contents, Scarisbrick remains an awesome monument.

From a distance, only the grim, fantastic tower rises over the trees, echo of the elder Pugin's involvement in Big Ben. From the drive, the difference between father and son is evident. To the left is the façade which the elder Pugin applied to the earlier house. A solid Gothic porch fronts the Great Hall with bay windows to its left. The Great Hall's roof is crowned by a lantern. The style is studiously Perpendicular.

To the right of the entrance is the wing and lofty tower erected by E. W. Pugin. It is as if he were eager to outgun anything his father might have achieved. A Gothic riot appears to have broken out. The architecture is now effusive, enriched with turrets, niches and statues. An octagonal stair-tower is crowned with giant birds flapping their wings as if to escape. The tower is twice the height of what the elder Pugin apparently intended.

What survives inside today makes even more tragic what must have been lost in the course of the 20th century. The Great Hall is an epic of Gothic revival. Overhead are arches and wind-braces, painted and graceful. For once A. W. N. Pugin has created a roof of compelling strength and dignity.

To the left of the Great Hall is the Oak Room, its fittings too embedded to be removed by saleroom vandals. This is among the richest 19th-century rooms in England. Every inch of wall has carved panels, mostly of biblical scenes. The chamber is designed to glow with flickering medieval candlelight.

Next door, the King's Room is a Tudor Gothic chamber, a foretaste of A. W. N. Pugin's Palace of Westminster. Gothic panels fill the ceiling, and kings and queens the walls, framed by Gothic pilasters and tracery.

In the Red Drawing Room is a fireplace in which Gothic merges into Renaissance. A picture appears to celebrate Charles Scarisbrick, his mistress and children in front of the house. What is imported carving and what is by the elder Pugin is hard to tell. The decorative colouring in this and most of the rooms is by J. G. Crace, the AS initials suggesting it was executed for Anne.

Smithills Hall is a house of two parts, one Victorian (right), the other medieval (left). The earlier building dates back to the 1300s while the 19th-century ranges were designed in the 1870s by George Devey, eminent architect of Victorian 'cottage style'.

✦✦✧ Medieval house with Victorian wing by George Devey

2 miles NW of Bolton; museum, open part year

A path from the stables leads over a ravine through thick trees to where the old house of the Radcliffe family lies along a ridge. It was here that the Protestant, George Marsh, was investigated and burned during the Marian persecution in 1554. He stamped his foot on a flagstone at the entrance to the withdrawing room to assert his faith, the imprint remaining visible to this day. In 1801, the house was acquired by a family of Bolton bleachers, the Ainsworths. They commissioned George Devey to remodel and extend the old hall house with a wing and interiors in the style of William Morris. The building is now run by a local trust. Since entry is via the institutionalized Victorian wing, visitors should ask to be guided blindfold to the old rooms.

The Great Hall is older and smaller than the Lancashire norm. Its timbers date, according to local

Smithills hall

archaeology, from before 1350. The partition between hall and service wing, with four arched openings, is a virtuoso display of local carpentry, one tier of trefoils then one of quatrefoils rising to the open roof like giant scissors. This idiosyncratic style clearly dominated Lancashire architecture for a full two centuries. At the family end the timbering is simpler but behind is a rare 'bower' or downstairs parlour, complemented by a solar upstairs. The floor of the latter is rough with adze marks. The rooms have 17th-century furnishings and are well done.

In 1537, more rooms were added to form a new wing beyond the bower. Although much restored by the Victorians, they retain the intimate atmosphere of the 16th century. The withdrawing room has rich linenfold panelling, to Pevsner the finest in the county, and a frieze with heads facing each other in medallions. These are supposedly members of the Barton family, owners of the house at the time.

The balancing victorianized wing of Smithills contains the rooms converted and extended by Devey. They include the Green Room and the library, both darkly Jacobean. The library, with its caged books and inlaid overmantel, is strongly reminiscent of William Morris's work.

Speke hall

★★★★★ An Elizabethan mansion with sympathetic Victorian additions

At Speke, 6 miles SE of Liverpool centre; National Trust, open part year, grounds open all year

Has any house suffered greater humiliation? An airport roundabout places Speke Hall as an afterthought to Arrivals and Departures. Runways thunder east and west of the old timbers. Even the River Mersey at the end of the garden seems defeated and inert. When Liverpool decided to build its airport next to the Hall – and, originally, even took its name – the temptation to move it to a more kindly spot must have been overwhelming.

'... a black-and-white palace

amid pleasing lawns and generous trees ...'

Yet Speke sits defiant in incongruity, a black-and-white palace amid pleasing lawns and generous trees, shielding it from the roar of jets. The house was built by the Norris family during the 16th century, an arch declaring it finished in 1598. In 1795 it was sold to the Watt family, who restored it and rented it in 1867–77 to Frederick Leyland, Liverpool shipping tycoon and patron of Morris, Rossetti and Whistler. The house was later bequeathed back to any surviving Norris as a remarkable gesture by Adelaide Watt in 1921. Twenty years later, it passed to the National Trust, following a secondary clause in the will.

Speke is one of the most developed, and complete, examples of a moated courtyard house of its period. Four ranges sit round a small court in which stand two ancient yews, Adam and Eve. Inside

Above The dining room was created by Frederick Leyland out of two smaller rooms after his family found the Great Hall too draughty for mealtimes. The sandstone fireplace surround was copied from a 17th-century original found in the ruins of Old Hutt, at Halewood. **Right** The Great Hall has two bay windows; in the north bay hangs a full-length portrait of John Middleton, a local farmer known as 'The Childe of Hale', who was born in 1578. Middleton achieved fame on account of his great height – it was said he was more than nine feet tall before he was twenty – and even attended the court of James I in 1620.

the court, the four façades are remarkably consistent, of herringbone timbering set on a sandstone plinth with a dazzling display of quatrefoil above. On two of the ranges and on both floors are continuous rows of windows overlooking the court, a cloister effect that renders the house picturesque both within and without. This is English domestic architecture at the limits of its ingenuity before succumbing to the Renaissance.

Inside, the house is strongly Victorian. The Watts and their tenant, Leyland, were medieval enthusiasts, happy to combine old with 'olden'. The rooms are full of de Morgan tiles, Pre-Raphaelite pictures and Morris wallpapers. Yet it is more old than new. The desire for authenticity at Speke is palpable. To wander these corridors and chambers is to immerse oneself in a past whose moment in time seems immaterial.

Of the chief rooms, the Great Hall is the star. It is an extraordinary chamber, almost square, its main timbers felled in 1530. By that time, a hall was for display rather than for merse oneself in **a past whose moment in time** seems immaterial.'

eating. It has two large bay windows flooding it with light, one with its own fireplace. Most remarkable is the Great Wainscot. Sporting carved busts, it rises to a jettied cornice crowded with black-and-gold enrichment. Nobody knows from where it came. The screens passage is no less curious, located behind a giant stone fireplace festooned with antique armour. It is a majestic space.

The Great Parlour is set at right angles to the hall and dates from the same period as the Great Hall. A later Jacobean ceiling is coated in beautiful floral plasterwork. Over the fireplace are portrayals of the Norris family, as if they were weepers on a tomb chest. The carving has the appearance of spun barley sugar. The room has been refurnished in Victorian style.

The rooms along the west side of the court all reflect Leyland's occupancy. His particular contribution was in replacing most of the fireplaces in an artistic manner. The dining room has a delightful Dutch-tiled overmantel and fire surround copied from a house demolished for the Halewood car factory. The library is suitably cluttered with rich leather books and Morris wallpaper. Another Leyland room is beyond the hall, the charming Blue Drawing Room, its grate decorated with sunflowers.

The upper galleries at Speke would have served as Long Galleries in more compact houses. Light floods into panelled corridors, fortuitously aligned so the noise of the adjacent airport is dampened.

Above left The Oak Bedroom is furnished as it was during the time of Adelaide Watts, who inherited Speke in 1865 while still a child. She lived at the hall after the Leyland's tenancy ended in 1877 until her death in 1921. An unproven rumour that Charles I stayed here in 1630 lead to this room being known occasionally as the Royal Bedroom. **Above** The library was created by Leyland out of a former scullery. He framed the corner fireplace with elongated columns derived from similar examples in the Great Hall; the tiles around the grate are of local origin. The walls are hung with one of William Morris's earliest wallpaper designs, 'Pomegranate', first printed in 1864.

Stonyhurst

★★ Elizabethan house with later additions, now a famous school

4½ miles SW of Clitheroe; private house, open part year

Most great recusant houses started as Roman Catholic and became less so. Stonyhurst has become more so. One of the most splendid Elizabethan houses in the North, it is now a leading Catholic school run by the Jesuits. The building is reached along a drive that passes through the village and grows in confidence until it reaches a huge statue of the Virgin Mary. It then puffs out its chest, turns right and charges towards the massive pile on the hill. For a small boy on his first day at school, it must be terrifying.

'One of the most **splendid Elizabethan houses** in the North...'

The old house was built in 1592 by Sir Richard Shireburne, variously spelt, on land that his family had occupied since the 13th century. He clearly built to impress, but not for long. The family's Catholic and Royalist sympathies brought them scant prosperity in the 17th century. The quadrangle behind the tower gatehouse was never completed. The house passed by marriage to the Weld family of Dorset and when Thomas Weld heard that his old Jesuit school at Liège had been closed by Napoleon, he offered Stonyhurst as a refuge. It has been the headquarters of the English Jesuits ever since.

The approach up the half-mile avenue is flanked by beautifully landscaped canals. The gatehouse is adorned with cupolas added in 1712, the effect enhanced rather than diminished by the collegiate ranges extending on both sides. The large 19th-century chapel was copied from King's College, Cambridge.

Shireburne's gatehouse at Stonyhurst is one of the grandest of its period in the country, carrying a full four storeys of classical orders. Inside, the courtyard is overpoweringly medieval, almost sinister. The hall lies ahead; its entrance has gone but the three-storey bay window survives. The right range was converted, with a new doorway, by Sir Nicholas Shireburne in a short-lived burst of Catholic enthusiasm under James II. The left range is Victorian. In a gloomy northern dusk this might be a prison courtyard.

The inside is inevitably institutionalized. The Great Hall has become the school Refectory, with a thinly ribbed ceiling and modest fireplace. It is hung with pictures of Jesuit masters and old-boy VCs, heroes of mind and body. The stained glass recalls champions of money, the great Catholic dynasties educated at the school.

A series of undercrofts beneath the hall has been converted into an admirable museum of the school's history. Thomas Weld is rightly honoured along with the customary school relics, the more exotic because of its continental past. Of Sir Nicholas Shireburne's Stuart range, the Duke's Room retains an original floral frieze. The finest space is the Victorian staircase, uniting old house and later school with panache.

Turton tower

★ ☆ Medieval pele tower with Victorian extensions

At Turton, 4 miles N of Bolton; museum, open part year

Turton Tower is an old house run as an informal, slightly dotty museum in the care of Lancashire County Council. Such custodianship is normally a disaster. Not here. The house was inhabited by the Orrells and the Chethams before being restored 'in the olden style' by the Kay family after 1835. It was the local town hall from 1930 to 1974. From all this it has recovered. The stone is warmed by Virginia creeper. The rooms show no trace of municipalization and little museumitis. Some even contrive to look inhabited.

Turton is in the northern tradition of pele tower and Tudor additions. The difference is that here the 15th-century tower is wholly dominant, the black-and-white extensions clinging like parasites. The extensions are not all they seem. Most are a 19th-century wrapping for what was a free-standing cruck house, now encased in Jacobethan gables.

The entrance is at the foot of the battlemented tower through a two-storey porch of 1592. Beside it is a much-altered stair turret of the same date, its own porch covered in rich quatrefoils. The rest of what is visible is attractive but early Victorian, with oversailing, herringbone timbering and bargeboards, a sort of 'chalet Lancastrian'.

The rooms are greatly enhanced by being an approved outpost of both the Victoria & Albert Museum and the National Portrait Gallery. The downstairs hall thus has a lovely Gothic chest, a suit of armour and Pugin wallpaper. The adjacent dining room, in the pele tower, is a Victorian re-creation of a 17th-century interior, installed by the Kays in the 19th century.

The drawing room upstairs would have been the pele tower's Great Hall and was later used as Turton District Council chamber. The room was therefore never far from the centre of local power. Panelling, ceiling and internal porch have all been restored to their 1590s state. The Tapestry Room contains the V&A's Courtenay Bed of 1593, a masterpiece of late Elizabethan design, with astonishing scrolled bases to its posts and intricate canopy carvings. It had been at Turton for much of the 19th century. In another room is a German overmantel of the *Last Supper*; the disciples are sitting round a huge chicken. Upstairs can be found a V&A wardrobe by Ashbee and a chair by Rossetti. This is where such objects should be housed.

The rooms within the cruck-framed wing remain in their 16th-century condition. The cruck uprights are visible in some of the walls. The top of the tower has been seized for a museum.

'The stone is warmed by Virginia creeper.'

Wythenshawe hall

✦✧ Former Tatton-family seat with ornate Tudor interiors

At Northenden, 6 miles S of Manchester centre; museum, open part year

Any attempt to disentangle the relations between the Tattons (or Egertons) of Wythenshawe and the Egertons (or Tattons) of Tatton is doomed to confusion. Like the Leghs and the Davenports of Cheshire, the big families of old Lancashire inter-married and sought deed polls to protect their entails. Suffice that the first recorded Tatton was in 1290 and the last, Robert Tatton, died in 1962.

Manchester Corporation tried to buy the Wythenshawe estate compulsorily in the 1920s for housing. The family bitterly resisted, pointing out that being besieged and 'reduced' by Cromwell was surely punishment enough for their wealth. In 1926, however, the fight had gone from them and 2,500 acres were indeed sold. The house and park were bought by the Manchester tycoon and benefactor, Lord Simon, and donated to the city corporation for public use. The old family chauffeur was retained to serve teas. The two Tatton heirs died, one as a boy at Eton and the other in the Second World War. Their father died in 1962 and the line ended.

Above The walls of the withdrawing room at Wythenshawe were once painted with *trompe l'œil* panelling, imitating the wood-lined halls of other Tudor mansions. Above the fake panelling ran a frieze, intended to look like a plasterwork relief; a portion of this and some of the imitation panelling is all that remains of the painted decoration. The mermaid-like figure supports a coat of arms that commemorates the marriage, *c*1580, of Dorothy Booth of Dunham Massey to William Tatton.

The house presents a conventional Tudor entrance front, heavily victorianized. Wings, gables and a turret have been added, making the survival of the house's medieval core the more remarkable. The Great Hall has dark red walls and is superbly panelled, with delicate Renaissance details. On the stairs is a sympathetic painting of a Commonwealth soldier being taunted by Royalist troops.

The old chapel, converted into the Chapel Bedroom, has its original coved ceiling, fireplace and Tudor bed with a charming crib beside it. Another bedroom has a bed with caryatids holding its tester and bold Renaissance panels. In the library is a painting of *The Old Squire*, symbolizing the constancy and family pride in place that sustained these houses through many centuries of change – only to be defeated by the 20th.

Stafford

shire

Casterne Hall

Staffordshire

Alton castle

⭐ Fantasy castle by Pugin on bluff above a ravine

At Alton, 5 miles N of Uttoxeter; private house, open by arrangement

The Earls of Shrewsbury were England's answer to Ludwig of Bavaria, creating their castles above the ravine of the River Churnet. Alton Towers, designed by the young A. W. N. Pugin, was intended as the 16th Earl's family home. The purpose of this second house a mile down the valley, also by Pugin, changed during construction. It looks as if it were designed for a Wagnerian princess, seized with a fit of piety.

The castle is a Rhineland Gothic fantasy of towers, turrets and steep roofs. It soars on a rock across the ravine separating it from the Hospital of St John. This is a Catholic school, house and almshouse, part of the same settlement.

The exterior to the courtyard is that of an L-shaped crenellated mansion, but with tower and the chapel piled up behind, as if to stop it sliding downhill. The chapel roof is in vivid yellow and green tiles. The polygonal apse dominates the skyline from the valley.

The castle is now a Catholic youth centre and a polite request is needed to gain entry, although the outside is impressive enough. The principal room is the chapel. This is an extension of the central hall, a bizarre arrangement for any home. The hall is Puginian, brightly painted and rising past a gallery to a lantern. It serves as a foyer to the chapel, the whole interior being emphatically ecclesiastical. It really should be more accessible.

Alton towers

✦ ✧ Ruined 19th-century Gothic palace at heart of the theme park

Near Alton, 6 miles N of Uttoxeter; private house, theme park open part year

Where to begin? Alton Towers is today a ruin, a grotesque and melancholic Castle Grim and backdrop to a shamelessly inappropriate theme park and fun fair. The creeper-encrusted walls of the old house gaze down at the plastic boats on the lake, across which are a fake village street, fast-food outlets and roller-coasters. 'I don't go near the place, it's spooky,' said the ticket lady when I asked if the ruin was accessible. Yet spookiness is the saving grace of Alton, defying the surrounding vulgarity. This is truly a place of Goths. The great-aunt from Transylvania may be a corpse but her eyes are still open. She will be there still when the rest has vanished.

Alton Towers was built for two Talbots, both Earls of Shrewsbury, from 1810 onwards. The bulk of the house was begun for the 15th Earl to designs possibly by James Wyatt and others. A series of architects laid out the gardens along the contours of the Churnet valley, filling them with exotic structures. At this stage, all was normal Regency Picturesque. The 16th Earl succeeded in 1827 and moved up a gear. In 1837 he imported the toast of the Victorian Catholic aristocracy, the twenty-five-year-old Augustus Welby Pugin, and proceeded to transform his uncle's house. Like Scarisbrick Hall (see page 136) and Carlton Towers, in Yorkshire, Alton was to embody Catholic Romanticism.

The house is the more impressive the nearer one gets. It is accessible to the public visiting the theme park, and refreshingly empty. The roof has been restored and stairs give access to upper floors. Of Pugin's own interiors, the Great Banqueting Hall, forming the spine of the house, and the chapel interior survive. The former has two magnificent Gothic fireplaces. Hardman glass survives in the bay window. The chapel has also been restored, with modern stained glass. Otherwise one can walk along passages and enter the shells of the drawing room, gallery and music room. Remains of the walls survive in the library and in an alcove called the Poets' Corner. Stripped brick vaults echo with the ghosts of medieval entertainment.

The theme park owners are trying slowly to restore more of the rooms. The upper rooms are accessible and give splendid views over what was once the park. To the rear is a wide grassy courtyard with ruined domestic offices. This place needs only a modern Pugin and a modern Shrewsbury.

Barlaston hall

★★ Palladian villa set in the Potteries

At Barlaston, 3 miles N of Stone; private house, open part year

The house sits lonely on a hillside overlooking the River Trent. Its proximity to the Wedgwood works suggests the residence of a Potteries magnate but this is not so. It was completed in 1756 for a Leek lawyer, Thomas Mills, on marrying a local heiress, Ester Bagnall, in 1742.

Mills's architect was almost certainly Robert Taylor, recently returned from the Grand Tour. The style is that of a Palladian villa and must have seemed tall and sophisticated in a landscape of Jacobean manors and scruffy industrial workings. It seems no less sophisticated today.

From the outside, the house is unusually plain. The plan is cruciform, of four large reception rooms set round a central staircase hall, rising the full three floors of the house. The rooms are occupied privately by the Hall family and are still being restored.

The rescue of Barlaston in the 1970s was a cause célèbre of the lobbying group, SAVE Britain's Heritage. The house had been stripped even of its fireplaces by the Coal Board, whose subsidence had apparently doomed it to collapse. It was bought from the original owners, Messrs Wedgwood, for £1. Coal Board compensation paid for a lengthy programme of restoration.

Chief discovery was Taylor's elaborate Rococo plasterwork. His motif of octagonal lozenge shapes is everywhere. They appear in window frames, panelling, plasterwork, even bookcases. In the course of salvage, other rich Baroque and Rococo designs have emerged, a product of Taylor's Italian studies. In the dining room, the picture frames, roundels and overmantel are all of Rococo design. The saloon is lit by a large sweeping bow and has a plasterwork frieze.

The library bow window has roundels of Shakespeare and, now, of John Betjeman, hero of the conservation movement to which we owe the survival of this house.

Casterne hall

⭐ Georgian house overlooking the Manifold valley

Near Ilam, 4 miles NW of Ashbourne; private house, open part year

The village of Ilam is the most picturesque in the Staffordshire Peak area. Its old hall is now a Youth Hostel, but a road up the isolated valley beyond reveals an apparition. Round a fold in the moors is a stylish 18th-century façade that might be in the centre of Derby. In front are a wall, posts and steps hinting at a long-lost courtyard. Behind is a rough-and-tumble farmyard.

The house is that of the Hurt family and its hindquarters show it to be of some antiquity. Massive rubble walls conceal a maze of blocked doors, windows, arches and odd angles. The front is Queen Anne in style though Georgian in date, 1730. The front door is a lovely composition, rusticated with a pedimented window above.

The house inside is still being restored. The hall has a fine stone fireplace with a vaguely Baroque curve to its mantelpiece. The Oak Room has imported panelling of *c*1610. With each phase of repair, a new discovery is made. This is a house whose past is still in its future.

Chillington hall

★★★ Mansion with parts by Soane, set in Capability Brown landscape

Near Codsall, 6 miles NW of Wolverhampton; private house, open part year

There have been Giffards at Chillington since 1178. The present incumbent, who lives here with his Texan wife, is the former Chief Constable of Staffordshire. The house has been restored and the Giffards are now at work on the majestic 1,000-acre park. This seems in revolt. Its unruly trees and grass seem to be marching up to the foot of Soane's portico and challenging the family to return Chillington to Nature.

The Giffards were Midlands recusants who paid dearly for their faith. They arrived with William the Conqueror, served Henry VIII and turned spy on Mary Queen of Scots. Ardent Catholics, they joined the Penderels of neighbouring Boscobel, in Shropshire, in helping Charles II escape after Worcester. The family still act as trustees of the Penderel Pension, paid by Charles as a reward.

Giffards never gained national fame or nobility, preferring the quiet virtues of estate management. Their one celebrity came from an incident in the 16th century when a Giffard shot a panther that had escaped from his menagerie and was about to savage a mother and child. The panther was immortalized as the family crest in 1513, a bearded archer being added ten years later. The family motto is 'Take breath and pull strong'.

The house is approached along a mile of drive, magnificently landscaped by Capability Brown. Landscape buildings are by James Paine and others. Although sliced by the M54 and the Shropshire Union Canal, this wild park contrasts with the manicured landscape, also by Brown and Paine, at neighbouring Weston. A Grecian temple, possibly by Robert Adam, faces the lake, along with assorted temples, bridges, cottages, terraces and urns. All this is in process of repair.

'Soane's interiors **are spectacular** ...'

Right The Saloon is lit by a lantern, set above the room. Soane was to make use of top lighting again and again, particularly when a building's design meant that there could be no windows. At the Bank of England, begun in 1788, where the rooms were enclosed within a windowless perimeter wall for security reasons, Soane created top-lit interiors very similar to Chillington's Saloon.

The Giffards rebuilt their old Tudor courtyard house in two bursts of energy in the 18th century. The first is attributed to Francis Smith of Warwick but was probably by the local architect, Richard Trubshaw. The second was by the young Sir John Soane, who contributed the portico in 1786. Soane's architecture is not always loveable and his east wing, naked amid lawn and gravel, does not smile. Trubshaw's south front, built in 1724, is less austere, of redbrick with stone dressings. Soane had intended a complete rebuild, but was obliged to keep this wing. The poor join can be seen at the attic storey.

Soane's interiors are spectacular. The entrance hall with Ionic columns is as he designed it, in bright turquoise. The vivid colours displayed throughout Chillington, much to its advantage, are claimed to be original. The Soane front comprises a drawing room and dining room. The drawing room mirror is Soanian, crowned with the Giffard panther's head. The dining room contains two magnificent paintings by Batoni.

Behind the hall, Soane intended a family chapel where had been the Tudor Great Hall. Instead he created a saloon. This is the most exciting space in the house, reminiscent of Soane's lost chambers at the Bank of England in London. Wide Soanian arches support an elliptical cove to a lantern, which floods the room with light. The walls are again turquoise. The fireplace is a brutal neo-Tudor confection out of place in this room. It depicts, yet again, Giffard shooting the panther.

Beyond is the 1720s staircase hall and everything that Soane is not, sensuous and decoratively fussy. The stair treads are adorned with panthers. The wall panels contain busts and plasterwork in the style of Artari and Vassalli. The effect is overwhelmed by a 19th-century window depicting the heraldry of recusants who married Giffards. The morning room contains a stucco ceiling of swirling panels and a roundel of the Goddess of Architecture.

Clifton hall

★ Restored fragment of a Smith of Warwick house

At Clifton Campville, 5 miles NE of Tamworth; private house, open by arrangement

The chief exhibit in Richard Blunt's house is his collection of before-and-after photos. He and his wife are two of the country-house saints who devote themselves to bringing hope to hopeless houses. Blunt was defeated by Sinai (see page 172) and is rescuing Staunton Harold, in Leicestershire. Clifton is his own. It was designed by Francis Smith of Warwick for the Pye family in 1705. The great house was intended to fill the centre of the composition, with wings for the stables and kitchens. The main house was never built, only the wings. In c1720 one of these was altered to make a family house. The empty site in the middle is a walled garden, enclosed grass and a lonely cedar.

The two identical wing-houses were farm buildings, roofless and derelict when Blunt took them in hand in 1996. Vegetation had enveloped the walls. Tractors sat where shelter survived. Both wings have now been restored, one as the Blunts' home. They stand overlooking a field outside Clifton Campville. The material is pink brick with nip-and-tuck mortaring. So robust are the Midlands stone dressings as to have needed almost no repair.

Two magnificent doorways face each other across the court, with scrolly Baroque pediments embracing the Pye coat of arms. The windows have glazing bars and handmade glass, giving a lovely reflecting sheen to the façades. On one front English Heritage insisted that Victorian sash windows be kept as 'part of the building's history', stupidly spoiling Smith's symmetry. I suppose the formerly collapsed roof was also history.

There is not much to see inside. This is essentially a family home. The original kitchen retains its massive fireplace and storage cupboards. A fine oak floor has been reinstated on the ground floor. Every part of the interior is flooded with light from the 48 windows. Clifton shows that no historic building is beyond redemption. Blunt has an imitation Knyff drawing of Clifton as it would have been if completed. In a way it has been.

Ford Green hall

✦✦ Jacobean yeoman's house with 18th-century wing

At Smallthorne, 2 miles N of Stoke-on-Trent; museum, open all year

A certain desperation surrounds the few historic houses of the Potteries. Stoke is uncompromisingly dreary and Ford Green Hall is its oasis. Such houses seem relics of an alien civilization left stranded in a desert of roads, car dealers, factories, warehouses and interminable dingy terraces. This is industrial England on whose works Shelley might have invited us to look and despair.

Ford Green Hall is an excellent black-and-white, half-timbered building set in a valley between two Potteries' suburbs. The house was built in 1624 for a yeoman farmer, Hugh Ford. A new wing was added in 1734. The house continued in the Ford family into the 19th century, when it decayed until rescued after the Second World War. It is now a local museum.

The exterior has close-studded timber-work. There are lozenge panels and, over the porch, remarkable timbering imitating a staircase balustrade. Such work indicates both wealth and decorative flair. The porch carries the inscription of its maker, 'Ralph. Sutton. Carpenter'. The interior is conventionally medieval. The parlour, main hall and kitchen have contemporary furniture. The kitchen pets look lifelike.

The staircase walls retain rough timbering with adze marks to hold a plaster coating. Of the upstairs rooms the most charming is the study over the porch, furnished for late-night letter-writing. The best bedroom has a fine chest and a four-poster bed. The latter is left unmade, a stylistic quirk now considered obligatory by politically correct custodians.

Hoar Cross hall

⭐ A neo-Jacobean pile with 17th-century style gardens

At Hoar Cross, 7 miles W of Burton upon Trent; now a hotel

The Victorian, Hugo Francis Meynell Ingram, was a hunting addict. His ancestor founded the Quorn Hunt and he himself died young in the field in 1871. His wife, Emily, daughter of Lord Halifax, commissioned G. F. Bodley to design the splendid memorial church near the new house, into which she and her husband had not yet moved. She occupied the 70 rooms as a childless widow. The couple had already inherited Temple Newsam, in Yorkshire, from her father and were victorianizing its interior at vast expense. At Hoar Cross, they were starting from scratch. It was and is a gigantic pile, now a hotel and health centre.

The architect was Henry Clutton and the style is a dutiful neo-Jacobean. The severity is relieved by the three canted bays to the garden terrace, further softened by copious creeper. The entrance front echoes Halifax's Temple Newsam, with 48 chimneys and turrets crowned with cupolas. The chief exterior virtue of Hoar Cross is the magnificent garden laid out by Lady Emily along lines suggested by Francis Bacon in the 17th century and now admirably restored.

The interiors of Hoar Cross are lifted by the presence of G. F. Bodley, architect also of the house's chapel. The plasterwork ceilings are mostly by him, with wallpapers by his friend, William Morris. They are excellent. The library walls are of 'Spanish leather'. On the ceiling, each plasterwork petal and leaf has been picked out in coloured paint, as have the roses in the Long Gallery. The dining room pendants are in similarly virulent colours.

The hotel uses a photographic technique for its 'paintings'. I prefer the signed photos of visiting celebrities. Departing visitors are warned by a notice, 'Paradise is just behind you'.

Izaak Walton's cottage

★ Ancient farmhouse cottage, now angling museum

At Shallowford, 4½ miles NW of Stafford; museum, open part year

Walton never lived in this cottage. He was a Stafford man who became a prosperous merchant in the City of London. As a Royalist during the Commonwealth he found it politic to leave the City and go fishing. Rather than write on so dangerous a topic as biography or theology, he decided to write a book about angling. The masterpiece, *The Compleat Angler*, has not been out of print to this day.

Walton bought Shallowford Farm in 1655 and donated its revenues to the poor of Stafford, adding money for them to have coal at 'the hardest and most pinching time of winter'. The cottage was eventually sold in 1920 and opened by a charitable trust in 1924 as a small museum to Walton and to fishing. Although sandwiched between the main line railway and overbearing farm buildings, the timbered and thatched cottage, with its herb garden, is charming.

Inside, the downstairs parlour is furnished in 17th-century style. Izaak sits in wax surrounded by his fishing equipment. Upstairs is a museum of angling history and a small library. Everywhere are rods, lines, flies and stuffed fish, with copies of *The Compleat Angler* helpfully left open for visitors to read. The museum has a complete run of reels, from the 18th century to today.

Kinver Rock houses

★ Cave houses cut out of a sandstone cliff

At Kinver Edge, 4 miles W of Stourbridge; National Trust, open part year

The English have neither the inclination nor the geology to boast many troglodytes. But there are some rudimentary rock houses in Nottingham and Knaresborough. The best are carved into an outcrop of vivid red sandstone overlooking the village of Kinver. The rock is known as Holy Austin after a hermit who was reputed to have lived on or in it. The earliest historical reference is by an 18th-century traveller caught in a storm on Kinver Edge. He hurried down the 'tremendous steep slope to some smoke I saw issue from a romantic rock near the foot'. It was occupied by 'a clean and decent family'.

By 1861 there were eleven families living in the excavated rocks, over forty people on three separate levels. The top level included a three gabled brick house extension. Small gardens spread down the slopes towards the wood. Numbers declined with the closure of the local ironworks and by the Second World War there were just two families here, one in the proper house, the other in the entire lower level. The caves had internal and outside wells and were supplied with gas. They suffered from damp and still gather mould.

Today the gabled house has been rebuilt and is private. Most of the old dwellings have suffered from vandalism and collapse, a terrible comment on the local authority. But the three lower houses were restored by the National Trust in 1997 and two are now open to the public, although one is given over to Trust self-promotion and 'interpretive display', a curse of these small properties.

The other house, of just two rooms, has been re-created as it was when occupied by Mr and Mrs Fletcher in the early 20th century. A fire burns cheerily in the stove. The table is laid for tea. The walls have been sealed, as far as they can be, with limewash that allegedly had to be purchased from America.

Erasmus Darwin house

★ Town house of eminent scientist and polymath

Beacon Street, Lichfield; museum, open all year

Darwin was the supreme scientific innovator of his age. He expounded the theory of the survival of the fittest, of biological variation and of evolution. He wrote extensively, was influential and widely celebrated. To his contemporaries, the name of Darwin was everywhere synonymous with science. This Darwin was not Charles but his grandfather, Erasmus. Wandering through this shrine to the great man, one starts to wonder just how much credit Charles deserved. At very least, Darwin junior's *Beagle* discoveries were exercises in testing his grandfather's theories.

Darwin was an 18th-century polymath. After studying medicine in Edinburgh, he arrived in Lichfield in 1725 and became a successful doctor. He was a giant of a man, overweight and afflicted with smallpox scars. Everything fascinated him, from zoology to engineering. He was a prominent member of the Lunar Society of Birmingham, a group of Midlands scientists and engineers, and friend of Wedgwood, Arkwright, Watt, Priestley and Boulton. He invented a speaking machine, a potato plough, a steam carriage, an artificial bird and a copying machine so accurate that copy and original could not be told apart.

Darwin was also a writer and a poet. He expressed the 'loves of the plants' with erotic accounts of stamens and pistils. His poem 'The Botanic Garden' caused a sensation. His theory of evolution was also set out as a poem, 'The Temple of Nature'. He even foretold Birmingham's motor age: 'Soon shall they arm, Unconquer'd Steam afar,/ Drag the slow barge or drive the rapid car.' His reputation collapsed abruptly during the Napoleonic wars. The heroes fighting the barbaric French did not like being told they were descended from apes.

It was in the 1760s that Darwin and his first wife, Polly Howard, transformed the old medieval house near the cathedral. They added a new front of reception rooms, with four handsome Venetian windows. The interior has been badly mauled by health-and-safety fanatics and is afflicted with museumitis, including costly audio-visual kit, stripping some rooms of their 18th-century atmosphere. But Darwin's personality dominates all. He fills the house and is present in two of the rooms in waxwork. From the rear windows is a glorious view towards the close and the west front of England's loveliest small cathedral.

Johnson's birthplace

LICHFIELD

★ Childhood home of the great lexicographer

Breadmarket Street, Lichfield; museum, open all year

Dr Johnson loved two things, company and books. 'Sir,' he said, 'I am obliged to any man who visits me.' As for books, what better than to enter the house where he was born and find oneself in a second-hand bookshop, which is what it was in his day. Michael Johnson, his father, was a man of books.

The house was built in 1707, a handsome structure with columns on the ground floor, tall rooms and two further storeys with attic above. It passed through various hands and was opened by the local council as a museum in 1901. It now houses memorabilia not located in Johnson's own house in Gough Square, in London. There is a fine collection of prints and drawings and, in an upstairs study, a library with all his works.

That said, the museum is heavily didactic. Each room traces a different stage in Johnson's life, some as tableaux, some as wall placards. On the ground floor, behind the bookshop, is Michael Johnson in his bookbindery. In those

days a bookseller was everything – publisher, printer, binder and salesman. He was both businessman and craftsman. We see him here as the craftsman.

In the basement in the re-created kitchen is a delightful surprise, an effigy of the nine-year-old Johnson reading *Hamlet*. It is said that when he reached the ghost scene in the play, 'he suddenly hurried upstairs to the street that he might see people about him'. This was the time when, deep in his books, he refused to help his sick father by attending his bookstall at neighbouring Uttoxeter market. The incident so weighed on his conscience that, fifty years later, he went to the same market and stood silent in the rain as an act of filial penance.

The rooms on the upper floors, in one of which Samuel was born in 1709, are mostly galleries of pictures, bindings and memorabilia. Johnson's true memorial is the books that fill the place. 'You can never be wise,' he said, 'unless you love reading.'

Moseley old hall

★★☆ Historic hall house with Royalist connections

4 miles N of Wolverhampton; National Trust, open part year

Moseley presents an image of a desperate and bedraggled Charles II, aged just twenty-one, arriving with a few friends at the back door in the early hours of 8 September 1651. His army had been annihilated at the Battle of Worcester.

The owner of the house, Thomas Whitgreave, was a known Catholic, and he and his priest, Father Huddleston, hid the young man from Parliamentary troops combing the area. Two days later, Whitgreave watched him depart, disguised as a servant, heading not for London and the throne but for Bristol and escape to France. Every moment of the incident was recounted by the King to Samuel Pepys and confirmed by Whitgreave. On Charles's Restoration nine years later, Whitgreave was given a pension of £200 a year and dubbed 'the Preserver'.

Whitgreaves lived at Moseley until 1820. The old house was then encased in Victorian brick, which saved it from collapse but spoiled its black-and-white exterior. It passed to the National Trust in 1962. The subsequent refurbishing of Moseley is one of the Trust's most successful exercises, giving it the warm embrace of Jacobean domesticity. A fire burns in the hall grate, herbs hang from rafters, dogs roam and Catholics pray.

Entrance is through the back door, claimed as the one on which King Charles knocked that famous night. The brewhouse is furnished as a kitchen. So immaculately displayed are the contents –

'Upstairs at Moseley is **a wonderfully secret place.'**

Above The chapel at Moseley Old Hall is a simple room, the walls are painted with *trompe l'œil* panelling and the altar is just a table, covered with a cloth. Father John Huddleston, recounting the events surrounding Charles II's stay at Moseley, claimed that the monarch had asked to see the room and praised it as 'a very decent place'.

herbs, peppers, spices, dried fruits – as to serve for a Dutch still life. The hall and parlour are cosy and filled with panelling, dark floorboards and old portraits and pewter.

Upstairs is the bed in which Charles slept. It was sold to Wightwick Manor in 1913 but sent back by the owners on Moseley's restoration. In the floor of the garderobe is the trapdoor of the hiding place in which Charles was hidden. He declared it 'the best place I was ever in'.

A corridor outside is hung with pictures and prints of Charles's escape. Mr Whitgreave's room is a panelled parlour filled with 17th-century furniture and much scrollwork and barley-sugar legs. It gives onto the intimate study from which Whitgreave is said to have watched Charles's supporters straggle down the lane for their long and dangerous walk back to Scotland.

The attic contains a small oratory chapel, with barrel-vaulted ceiling and star painting on its small celure. The chapel was used for services until a century ago. The priest's bedroom is next door and the roof contains many priest's holes. Upstairs at Moseley is a wonderfully secret place.

The garden reflects the same 17th-century intimacy as the interior. The National Trust has sought to re-create the topiary work, paths, alleys and knot gardens of the period. Flowers are self-consciously English. Trees are cherry, quince, mulberry and medlar. The sense of seclusion is marred only by the passing M54. Perhaps one day we can devise quieter engines and quieter tarmac.

Sandon hall

★ ★ Neo-Jacobean mansion by William Burn

At Sandon, 5 miles NE of Stafford; private house, open by arrangement

Such are the demands of country-house economics that Sandon must call its attractions 'exclusive' and its dining room 'a setting for prestige dinner parties'. There is force in the exclusive. To gain entry I had to brave a fierce blue tit guarding its young nesting in the mouthpiece of the entrance security telephone. Lord Harrowby defends his territory in style.

The house is grey, stern and Victorian, as rebuilt after a fire by William Burn in 1852. Burn was master of Jacobean Revival and Sandon is a virtuoso display. Giant banks of rhododendrons and azaleas line the drive from the main road. Cedars rise in a glorious crescendo.

The entrance façade is a symmetrical E-plan with central *porte-cochère* crowned by turrets. Windows have fiddly strapwork and quoins are like leather straps. The interior is virile neo-Jacobean, recalling Burn's work at Harlaxton, in Lincolnshire. Most magnificent is the hall, divided by two screens of columns, the walls scarlet and the panelling dark wood. At the end is a fine staircase rising and returning in two flights to the landing. It seems designed for a cavalier to come galloping down the hall and sweep a damsel off her feet. Angelica Kauffmann depicts three Harrowby girls as *The Three Graces*.

The state rooms are heavy. Burn's giant pendants drip like stalactites over the guests below. Learning does not sit light on the library, weighed down with books and busts. The drawing room has hand-painted Chinese wallpaper, clearly older than the house. A magnificent conservatory was added in 1864. It too is bombproof Victorian.

Shugborough

★★★ Wyatt mansion with park by James 'Athenian' Stuart

4 miles NW of Rugeley; National Trust, open part year

Some houses start with a place, others with a person. Shugborough starts with two brothers, Thomas Anson who inherited the house in 1720, and his younger brother, George, who became England's most celebrated 18th-century admiral. George sailed round the world for four years, during which he captured a Spanish galleon out of Acapulco, the *Nuestra Señora de Covadonga*, which carried £400,000 in gold, a stupendous sum. These English sea captains were little short of privateers. Anson's share of the money paid for his brother's rebuilding of Shugborough.

Thomas's first task was the garden, intended to rival that of Stowe, in Buckinghamshire. He commissioned James 'Athenian' Stuart to dot the park with classical monuments, including a triumphal arch, Doric temple and Tower of the Winds. In among them wandered Corsican goats. Poussin was to be reincarnated in the glades of Staffordshire on the profits of Spanish gold.

As for the house, Thomas Anson added wings to the old William-and-Mary building, and filled it with excellent plasterwork by Vassalli. This 1740s house was converted by a great-nephew, Viscount Anson, between 1790 and 1806, to designs by Samuel Wyatt, brother of James.

Wyatt turned a lively vertical house into a severe horizontal one, early Georgian into late Georgian. A colonnade united the central block with one pavilion with domed bow windows on either side. (The domed bow is a Samuel signature.) The outside he covered in grey dressed slate, a smart but cold material even when polished to look like the finest ashlar.

There is nothing cold about the interior. The family is now represented by a guide, acting the part of Viscount Anson, who welcomes visitors to the main reception rooms. More guides, all

Above When Shugborough was extended c1748, the present library was created by linking two rooms, one old and one new, through an archway cut in the outside wall of the 17th-century house. Royal photographs dotted around the room remind visitors that the famous photographer and cousin of the Queen, Patrick Lichfield, lived here until his death in 2005.

appropriately costumed, people the house and grounds, taking on the roles of early 19th-century servants. Each character is based upon contemporary estate records of real people.

The rooms contrast classical severity with flashes of Baroque ostentation. The first rooms on the ground floor display Greek and Roman antiquities. The north wing ends in the dining room, with a fitted set of scenic paintings of Bologna, believed to have been painted in the 18th century. The chimneypiece has a picture of the Admiral in most unnautical robes. The enormous Red Drawing Room is Samuel Wyatt's most accomplished work, of 1794 in the Adam style.

Wyatt built the great saloon to receive the Prince Regent, who never came. Next door, a billiard room includes a Rococo ceiling brought from the old Chinese House in the grounds. It is a charming confection of oriental motifs in Italian settings. Also here is a set of Chinese porcelain given to George Anson in thanks for his sailors extinguishing a fire during a visit to Canton.

The last, and most intimate, of the public rooms is the library. This is in two parts, divided by a Soanian arch with columns and niches, penetrating the wall of the original house. Although formal in architecture, the two rooms are pleasantly cluttered with books, magazines and photographs of the Royal Family. Mirrors make it look as if the books go on for ever.

The estate is run by Staffordshire County Council in collaboration with the National Trust. This is a well-presented house, despite the perils inherent in co-management.

Sinai house

Restoration is hardly the word for what Kate Newton is doing to this romantic ruin on a wild bluff overlooking Burton upon Trent. Drivers on the A38 see a gaunt skeleton on the horizon, of a roof collapsed in what seems a derelict farm. Close to, we can discern a medieval E-plan coming back to life, with help from copious grants and total dedication.

The house was an outpost of a Burton monastery of *c*1500. It passed to the Paget family at the Dissolution, who added a central hall range to create the present house. This became a farmhouse but was wrecked by the RAF, worst of the Services in abusing houses during the Second World War. Salvaged as six cottages, the house was then used as a barn. The local authority took no action to stop it collapsing, until eventually the great oak beams of the roof fell and ruined the interior wall-paintings. The place was, and still is, dangerous. Only its isolated location can have saved it from the bulldozer.

Miss Newton acquired Sinai in 1994 and she and her partner have rebuilt and occupied one wing, with meticulous conservation of surviving details, including fragments of the wall-paintings. The new oak staircase is by Venables of Stafford. The rest remains to be done when funds permit. The house is moated, with a small 18th-century bridge. These buildings need saints and Sinai is lucky to have found one.

'... this **romantic ruin** on a **wild bluff**.'

Stafford: Ancient High house

★★ Rich merchant's town house of the 16th century

Greengate Street, Stafford; museum, open all year

Elizabethan town houses were the skyscrapers of their age. Crammed onto a prominent central site, what is claimed as the 'largest timber-framed town house in England' glows with pride in the middle of Stafford. Less excusable is the desecration of the place by health-and-safety officials. They have taken a building that has resisted fire for four centuries and transformed it into a fire-door exhibition centre.

The building is positioned on a street corner. The close-studding of its timbers, the plethora of windows and the prominent chimney stacks all indicate wealth as well as strength. A Richard Sneyd lived here in the 17th century. The house was rebuilt in 1595 and the present rooms on display illustrate their occupancy over subsequent centuries. The staircase turret to the rear, rising three storeys, is a splendid timber structure.

The rooms are municipal-historical. The Civil War room was used to house Royalist prisoners 'of the better sort'. Others were tossed into the town gaol. Prince Rupert's dog is portrayed in wax. The Stuart bedroom has a fine Adam and Eve bed-head. There is a Victorian sitting room and an Edwardian office. The upper storeys turn to social history. The shop has real rather than wax fruit 'on sale'. There is a herb garden at the back.

Tamworth castle

★★ Norman castle with shell keep

At Tamworth, 7 miles SE of Lichfield; museum, open all year

The castle of the Marmions of Tamworth has failed to keep all enemies at bay. It is besieged on one side by tower blocks and on the other by shedlands. Even inside I fear that on a hot day it might become a pool of wax.

Yet this is a magnificent place. The castle passed from the medieval Marmions through the Ferrers in the 15th century to the Townshends in the 18th. In 1897, the Marquis Townshend sold it to the council for £3,000. The castle is a Norman motte-and-bailey, with a herringbone fragment of original wall surviving under the approach. The plan is of a shell keep, with fortified chambers tightly grouped round an inner courtyard.

The interior is medieval on the ground floor, with state rooms on the first and domestic rooms on the second. Under the tower is a dungeon (with wax prisoner). The banqueting hall, with a 15th-century roof, is reached through a fine Renaissance doorway. The state rooms are formed from an earlier Long Gallery.

A Jacobean gentleman rests on a sumptuous bed, entertained by a taped lutenist. Beyond is the dining room with florid overmantel. This, with other 17th-century features, was brought from Chislehurst in Kent during the castle's 19th-century 'jacobeanization'. The tablecloth appears in disarray and the bread looks admirably fresh.

The top floor rooms display the castle's last period of occupation under Townshend's tenants, the Cooke family, in the 1880s. We see the Cooke bedrooms, nursery, bathroom and the endearing clutter of a large Victorian family. Annie Cooke's room has a quilted counterpane and is enhanced by an effigy of her reading a book. The Cookes lived comfortably in their castle, proving that ancient structures can be well adapted to modern use.

A haunted bedroom has a video playing and an actress warns a waxen Lord Marmion to 'repent of your evil act', followed by a terrible wailing. This is surely meant for the local planning officer.

Trentham park

⭐ Remaining fragment of a great Victorian mansion

At Trentham, 3 miles S of Stoke-on-Trent; private garden, open all year

Here in the suburbs of Stoke could be a set for the surrealist cult film *Last Year in Marienbad*. A roundabout on the A34 advertises Trentham Park Gardens, a tatty 1960s conference centre attended by cafés and a car boot sale. Huts and prefabs abound. This might be former Eastern Europe.

Be not deterred. Buy a ticket and follow the directions over a bridge and through the bushes. Beyond lies a ghost. Even Pevsner had to abandon a strict rule 'not to describe buildings that have been demolished' to conjure up the pleasure dome of Trentham. It was designed by Sir Charles Barry for the 2nd Duke of Sutherland in 1833. The house had belonged in 1540 to James Leveson, one of the Duke's ancestors; it was rebuilt by Smith of Warwick and Henry Holland before the arrival of Barry.

For the 2nd Duke, Barry built an Italianate palace as spectacular as anything in the country, comparable with the similar Italianate house the same pair were creating at Cliveden, in Buckinghamshire. The Duchess had rightly rejected the original designer, Edward Blore, as 'that cheap architect'. Trentham was to cost £123,000. Almost everything was destroyed in 1912, when industrial pollution of the river forced the abandonment of the house. The site passed to a property company.

Remaining at present is the entrance colonnade and *porte-cochère*. A panel carries the Duke's coat of arms, a glimpse of former splendour. Behind is a lawn where the house lay, with the remains of the stables and clock-tower. A notice in front announces 'the largest formal garden in England', the work of William Nesfield. Here yew and box stand silent witness to the passing greatness of the place, as they do at Witley Court, in Worcestershire. The terracing has been repaired and glides down to the edge of the restored lake.

All this forms the setting for a new hotel planned on the site of the old mansion. At the time of writing, a developer promises a building with 'the scale' of Barry's. If he can find an architect fit for the task, well and good, but why not rebuild Barry? The present dereliction is a blot on the face of Staffordshire.

Oak house

★★ Late Elizabethan black-and-white mansion

Oak Road, West Bromwich; museum, open all year

West Bromwich needs all the historic buildings it can find. This one languishes in all its glory, a Cinderella amid the most depressing industrial squalor, even for the Black Country. I could find no trace of a sign anywhere near.

The black-and-white Midlands manor is dated *c*1600, despite the 1488 on a drainpipe. Pictures of the house before its restoration as a museum in 1898 show it as now, dominated by three wide gables and a fourth, close- studded, over the porch. More remarkable are the four colossal chimney stacks accompanying the black-and-white belvedere on the roof. This must have been intended as a look-out, a form much favoured by late-Elizabethan builders.

The interior is of a familiar plan, although the old screens passage has fallen foul of museumitis and the hall has had its ceiling removed. This is apparently to allow a view up to the look-out, which is pointless. The service wing is to the left, the parlour and solar to the right. These are excellently restored, panelled and with old beams and furniture of the period. In the dining room is a Tudor oak chair with carved back and sides. A 17th-century morning room has panelling with shelves, a dresser and a writing desk.

Upstairs is a warren of small bedrooms with four-posters and old flooring. One of the beds has original 17th-century needlework hangings, simple but charming. This is a delightful house, but does anyone know it is there? There was no guidebook on my visit.

Old Manor house

⭐⭐ Medieval manor complex with Elizabethan gatehouse

Hall Green Road, West Bromwich; public house, open all year

Visitors to this astonishing place are greeted with the promise of 'Button-bustin' Feasting and Merriment'. I would add, 'eye-poppin''. No sooner have the suburbs of the West Midlands anaesthetized the senses than round an anonymous bend is an apparition. A derelict 'old hall' surrounded by later clutter came on the market in 1950 and the local council found they had on their hands a 13th-century moated manor, complete with hall, courtyard, solar and chapel wing. They spent months trying to demolish it and then gave up. In 1957 a narrow majority decision was taken to restore it, with James A. Roberts as architect. The building was then rented to Ansell's Brewery as a pub.

The house has all the gaudiness of a Midlands eaterie. Muzak shrieks, fruit machines clatter, bars are crowded and 'merriment' utters from private rooms decked with medieval shields and banners. An armoured knight on a horse guards the buffet at the dais end of the hall. Yet there is nothing phoney about this building. It is the real McCoy. The moat has been dug out and filled with water. Unused corners, such as the medieval chapel, have been used for small displays of artefacts found on the site.

The courtyard is entered through an Elizabethan gatehouse. A tiny medieval courtyard lies inside with the entrance to the Great Hall ahead. This is open to the roof, a structure of c1290 supported on two massive cruck beams with rare double braces. All suggest a wealthy owner, believed to be William de Marnham, lord of the local manor in the 14th century. A pretty wooden screen with two ogee arches leads to the old service quarters (now another bar).

At the other end of the hall is a bay window alcove, and an excellent swooping canopy of honour above the now vanished dais. Behind this is the solar wing, with a Great Chamber almost as splendid as the hall. It has another open roof, its panels and frieze liberally stencilled and painted with medieval motifs and banners. A family gallery overlooks the two-storey chapel below. As far as I could see all this is original and admirably restored. I cannot object to these ancient halls re-employed as a raucous place of entertainment. That is what they always were.

Weston park

★ ★ ☆ Restoration mansion with Georgian additions by Paine

At Weston-under-Lizard, 7 miles E of Telford; private house, open part year

Weston Park is a splendid boast. It promises that 'royalty, politics, drama and tragedy' are part of its history. The facilities assure 'confidentiality and security'. Bill Clinton and Tony Blair had just signed the visitor book on my visit. A rock concert was departing the 1,000-acre park, to be followed by a country fair. The rooks in the surrounding woods mingled with the whistle of a miniature steam engine.

Given the pomp of its interior, the house is lucky to retain a jolly 17th-century outside. The house was built in 1671 by Lady Wilbraham, who possessed a heavily annotated 1663 edition of Palladio's *First Book of Architecture* and appears to have designed Weston herself. Unless we include Bess of Hardwick, she is possibly England's first woman architect. She placed bold segmental pediments on the south front wings. Her daughter and heir married into the Bridgeman family, later Earls of Bradford. It was this family that put the house into a charitable trust in 1981. The Earl of Bradford lives locally.

The entrance to the house was moved to the east front in 1865. It now goes into the former library, a fine chamber of classical columns and friezes. Weston has a superb picture collection, here devoted to horses. A 19th-century Earl of

Bradford was Master of the Horse to Queen Victoria. Beyond is the small breakfast room housing a set of Tudor and later portraits, including a Holbein.

At the heart of Elizabeth Wilbraham's house was an open courtyard, enclosed by the Victorians and refashioned as a hall and billiard room. These are now spaces for the display of pictures, sculptures and Chinese porcelain, including paintings by Bassano and Salvator Rosa. Weston also has a large collection of over 1,100 letters from Disraeli to the then Countess of Bradford, as well as a yellow parrot which he sent her. It was thought to be male, but laid 23 eggs and then dropped dead.

The main reception rooms are so heavily redecorated as to seem more 20th century than historic. The dining room is a shock. Scaled for giants, it was created in the 1860s by combining two rooms on the ground floor and more on the floor above. The new doorcases are thus higher than the old ones. Much of the opulent detail is the work of the 6th Earl's wife in the 1960s, including the hanging of rich pink wallpaper. The room is dominated by the pictures of Lely, Kneller, Dahl and a number of van Dycks. Most splendid is the portrait of Sir Thomas Killigrew,

'... the house is lucky to retain

Above The drawing room was designed by James Paine in 1760 and took the place of the original 17th-century entrance hall. It was redecorated in the 1960s by Lady Bradford, wife of the 6th Earl, and is hung with family portraits, many by Sir Peter Lely; his painting of Lady Elizabeth Wilbraham hangs between two windows, opposite the fireplace.

creator of the Theatre Royal and the first manager to put women on the stage. Weston should be a feminist shrine.

The present library is a mid-Victorian creation in classical style, with rich wood panelling and deep sofas. Fake books covering the doors include nine volumes of *The American Peerage*. To one side is a superb Indian lacquer screen bordered with Chinese characters promising long life. The room has two rare portraits by Constable and others by Reynolds, Hoppner and Hayter. Their colouring is as rich as the decoration.

The drawing room is emphatically 'a ladies' room'. It is by James Paine, who may have been responsible for much of the mid-Georgian work both indoors and outdoors at Weston. The main portrait here is a Lely of Lady Wilbraham,

looking most determined. An Anglo-Indian cabinet is faced in tooled ivory, decorated with charming oriental street scenes. The tapestry room is exquisite. Designed by Boucher for Gobelins, the tapestries of 1766 frame scenes by Watteau, Rubens and others. Birds take flight across a rich rose-tinted background. The furniture shrinks away in deference.

Weston has a large and formal set of stables and farm buildings built by Sir Henry Bridgeman, an enthusiast for 18th-century rural 'improvement'. The landscape, by Capability Brown, is still contained within a five-mile perimeter wall. Paine designed most of the Palladian landscape features, a bridge, obelisk, tower and summer house. Not far from the entrance stands his Orangery and linked Temple of Diana, a lovely folly.

a jolly 17th-century **outside.'**

Whitmore hall

★★ A house of medieval and Tudor parts, with Restoration and Georgian additions

At Whitmore, 4 miles SW of Newcastle-under-Lyme; private house, open part year

The hall stands delightfully positioned, enclosing the end of a long lime avenue from the parish church. At first sight, it seems conventionally William-and-Mary, with tall windows and steep pitched roof. Closer inspection reveals a rougher past, that of the Restoration and earlier. The windows are not the same. Huge chimneys poke rudely from behind a parapet. The Victorian porch looks tipsy. The Mainwarings, as politicians, soldiers, sailors or farmers in the Australian outback, claim to be celebrated for their drinking.

Whitmore defies historians. It has been in single family ownership since the Norman Conquest and the present Mainwarings have every intention of keeping it that way, 'planning authority and government' willing. The house was a medieval timbered E-plan encased in brick in 1676, and then given an 18th-century front and entrance hall. By this device, many an ancient English house was inexpensively transformed from medieval to 'modern'.

The rooms are light and bright, as of a comfortable Georgian house. Yet each springs a surprise. The guide, Mrs Cavenagh-Mainwaring, reveals lost Tudor walls, patches of lath and plaster, paperwork friezes and, under a table, a peacock found dead in the cellar. Fireplaces are lined with beautiful Minton tiles from the Potteries. The dining room with its ferocious family portraits looks like a warning against the demon drink.

Below the house by the stream are Elizabethan stables containing early 17th-century horse boxes. These are remarkable examples of equestrian architecture, though the form was common at the time. Each stall is arched and separated by a Doric column. They are earlier than those at another Mainwaring house at Peover (see page 43) of 1654. A number of horses perished here in a fire in the 18th century and no horse since has ever been induced to remain in the building overnight. Its survival is the more remarkable.

Wightwick manor

★★★☆ A Victorian-Tudor home with Arts-and-Crafts interiors

At Wightwick Bank, 3 miles W of Wolverhampton; National Trust, open part year

Wightwick is a Pre-Raphaelite banquet. Only a snooty Metropolitan would wonder at such a place existing in the provinces. There is nothing comparable in London, not even Leighton House. Here are the Pre-Raphaelites, William Morris and the Arts and Crafts movement immaculately displayed. Wightwick (pronounced Wittick) embodies the Victorian medieval revival.

Theodore Mander was a Wolverhampton paint and varnish manufacturer who married an American, suitably named Flora Paint. Mander was a follower of John Ruskin and Morris. He bought the Wightwick estate in 1887 and began six years of intense building and patronage, continued by his son, Sir Geoffrey Mander MP, and his wife, Rosalie Grylls. They amassed a collection of Pre-Raphaelite art when it was unfashionable and cheap. The house went to the National Trust in 1937 but the Manders maintained a flat upstairs and, until recently, their daughter Anthea lived there; she died in 2004. She wrote fiercely of Geoffrey and Rosalie as parents who 'discarded people but not things', and of 'emotional scars ... and painful memories'.

Wightwick was built in the Tudor style in two stages, six years apart. The earlier west wing is half-timbered with a brick ground floor. The more overtly antique east wing is in a timber-framed Cheshire style. Both are by Edward Ould, creator of 'Ould English'. He claimed that no other style would 'continue to live on terms of such good fellowship with other materials'. Our age of tawdry concrete and glass has proved him right.

Inside, the wallpapers, wall-hangings, fabrics and furniture are almost all by the William Morris Partnership, and are of great richness. Much of the stained glass is by Charles Kempe, signed with his wheatsheaf badge. De Morgan supplied tiles for the fireplaces and inglenooks. The latest electricity and central heating were installed. Walls are hung with paintings by Millais, Burne-Jones, Rossetti, Madox Brown, Watts, Ruskin and Leighton. Books on the shelves are bound by Morris's Kelmscott Press.

The older wing includes the drawing room with its Arts and Crafts furniture. Here is the celebrated portrait of Janey Morris with flowing red hair, begun by Rossetti but completed by Madox Brown. It hangs above a fine walnut-and-rosewood piano. The hall is lit with opaque glass in which are set Kempe's Virtues. The panelled library opposite, heavy with Hansards, also has Pre-Raphaelite glass.

The newer wing is more spectacular. It begins with the parlour, in effect a Great Hall. This revival of a medieval form was well described by Henry James in *The Other House*: 'Bright, large and high, richly decorated and freely used, full of corners and communications, it evidently played equally the part of a place of reunion and a place of transit.' The inglenook is a room in itself. Kempe decorated the ceiling and frieze panels with exotic animals in a forest. The walls are enlivened by Mander's noble

'Here are the Pre-Raphaelites ... immaculately displayed.'

Above left The night nursery at Wightwick was where the younger children of the household slept, watched over by their nurse. Now restored to its 1908 appearance, the nursery is decorated with a printed frieze of foxhound puppies, chasing ducks and chickens around the room. It was designed by Cecil Aldin, an artist and illustrator who specialized in characterful dogs. **Above** Wightwick Manor was the first house to be presented to the National Trust during the lifetime of its donor; Geoffrey Mander handed it over in 1937. The Manders continued to add to their collection after this date; the folding bed in the Oak Room, which came from the Putney home of poet Algernon Swinburne, was bought in 1939.

Above The entrance-hall windows are glazed with stained glass by Charles Kempe. In 1884, Theodore Mander attended a lecture by Oscar Wilde who urged his listeners to decorate their homes with only the finest craftsmanship. Inspired, Mander went on to furnish Wightwick with work by artists such as Kempe, William Morris and William de Morgan.

quotations. The room radiates colour, not least from Watts' portrait of Jane Hughes and Burne-Jones's medievalist icon, *Love Amongst the Ruins*, under the gallery. This is one of the finest rooms of late-Victorian England.

The rest of the wing is heavily neo-Jacobean. The billiard room has Morris Pimpernel wallpaper. Delft and Spode fill the dining room. The Pomegranate Passage is hung with a Burne-Jones tapestry of *The Mill*. Each of the visitors' bedrooms is designed to a decorative theme: Honeysuckle, Indian Bird, Acanthus and Daisy.

The Oak Room, with its linked dressing room and writing room, forms a perfect guest suite. The folding bed, contained within an ornamental cupboard, belonged to Swinburne. It opens to reveal not just a bed but a complete alcove, panelled, carved and painted. The ensemble cost six guineas in 1939. Today it must be priceless. Beyond are two delightful nurseries, day and night, with toys and dolls of all periods. Downstairs is a Turkish bath.

The garden is by Thomas Mawson, adapted by Geoffrey Mander. Such a layout, said Mawson, should become 'freer' the further it progressed from the walls of the house, as if nature were to be allowed slowly to take over from architecture. There is a plethora of topiary. On the lower lawn, the yews lead away from the house like a regiment of Cheddar cheeses.

Wolverhampton: Bantock house

★ Georgian house with late Victorian interiors

Finchfield Road, Wolverhampton; museum, open all year

Modern Wolverhampton may be a monument to the Unknown Traffic Manager, but the old town enjoyed men of a more subtle aesthetic. The Bantock family, father Thomas and son Baldwin, were mayors of Wolverhampton at the turn of the 20th century; their business was haulage. Like the Manders of Wightwick Manor (see page 181), they were patrons of the Arts and Crafts movement. In 1938, they donated their suburban home to the town for a museum. The downstairs has been restored as it would have been during family use.

Although the exterior is Georgian, the interior is mostly late Victorian. The entrance through the conservatory is into a dark panelled hall, decorated in the Arts and Crafts style. There are chairs of the period and a fine brass fireguard. Designs for stained-glass windows by Frederick Shields hang on the walls, facing a bold Art Nouveau lectern. The door hinges are beautifully crafted.

Facing the main entrance are portraits of the Bantocks in their mayoral robes, next to an incongruous suit of armour. To the left, in the dining room, is a japanned screen; this ancient lacquer technique was adapted by Wolverhampton craftsmen to fuse paint with tinplate, the source of the town's wealth.

To the right is the drawing room. Desks and books are still in place, together with beautiful chinaware and fireplace tiles. Wolverhampton's magnates were men of taste. The bay windows look out onto the Bantocks' treasured gardens; these have been restored to their original design.

Glossary

The aim in this book has been to avoid terms not familiar to the lay person. However, some specialist terms in common use in architectural circles may have crept in, for which the following may be helpful.

acanthus – pattern of an exotic Mediterranean flower with large leaves used in classical decoration.

anthemion – a honeysuckle flower pattern used in classical decoration.

Artisan Mannerist – buildings created by masons using pattern books (rather than architects) in the period c.1615–75. Mannerism originated in 16th-century Italy and was characterised by Classical elements used in unusual ways. It was taken up in the Low Countries, then spread to England.

ashlar – block of masonry fashioned into a wall, either load-bearing or to cover brick.

bailey, inner and outer – a fortified enclosure, usually moated and surrounded by a curtain wall, containing a motte (mound) with a keep on top. Walls are topped by battlements, with crenellations which protected defenders from arrows, and machicolations, or floor openings, through which attackers could be fired down on.

baluster – upright post supporting the handrail on stairs.

bargeboard – wooden board protecting the eaves of a roof.

bay – a space of wall between any vertical element, such as an upright beam, pillar or a division into a window or door.

bay window – window projecting out from a flat wall, either canted if the sides are straight, or bowed if curved.

bolection mould – moulding concealing the join of vertical and horizontal surfaces, shaped like an S in cross-section.

Boulle – elaborate inlay work on the surface of furniture, customary in 17th and 18th-century French work.

bow – see bay window

canted – see bay window

cartouche – frame for a picture or statue, often oval and surrounded by a scroll.

caryatid – a column in the shape of a draped female figure.

casements – see sashes

castle of enclosure – a form of early medieval castle in which individual buildings are enclosed within a curtain wall, in contrast to later medieval castles that consisted of a tower with subsidiary buildings in a courtyard to front or rear.

chinoiserie – a style of Rococo with Chinese motifs, often linked with Gothick.

coffering – a ceiling composed of beams enclosing sunken square or round panels.

collars – see roof timbers

corbel – a stone or wood projection in a wall that supports a beam, statue or sill.

cornice – (1) a ledge or projecting upper part of a classical entablature. (2) Moulding at the top of a wall concealing the join with the ceiling.

cottage ornée – late-Georgian/Victorian picturesque cottage, usually with thatched roof and Gothic windows.

crenellation – see bailey

crocket – Gothic decorative device, usually a cusp or curling leaf, at regular intervals on outer edges of spires, pinnacles and gables

cruck – a simple structure of two, usually curved, trunks of wood formed into an inverted V which support the walls and roof of a medieval house.

curtain wall – in castle-building, a wall constructed between defensive projections such as bastions.

dentil – one of a series of small square blocks along the base of a cornice

dorter – a sleeping room or dormitory, especially in a college or monastery.

dressing – a general term for finishings; stone is dressed to either a smooth or ornamental surface.

enfilade – a line of rooms in sequence along one side of a house, usually with interconnecting doors.

entablature – a feature of classical architecture comprising everything above column height, formally composed of architrave, frieze and cornice.

flatwork – decorative plaster or woodwork in low relief.

frontispiece – a decorative bay above a doorway in a Tudor or Jacobean building, customarily composed of Renaissance motifs.

gable – the triangular end of a double-pitched roof, sometimes with stepped or scrolled (Dutch) sides.

garderobe – privy or lavatory, usually discharging into a ditch or moat outside a medieval house.

Great Chamber – see solar

grisaille – monochrome painting, usually a mural and in shades of grey.

grotesque – decorative wall motif of human figures, as found in Roman grottoes.

half-timbering – term for timber-framed house derived from the practice of splitting logs in half to provide beams.

hipped roof – a roof with a sloping end instead of an end gable.

Ho-Ho bird – chinoiserie motif associated with 18th-century Rococo style.

jetty or jettied floor – upper floor extended, or oversailed, beyond the lower one to give more space upstairs and protect lower walls from adverse weather. Jettying also uses the downward thrust of the upper walls to form a cantilever, preventing internal ceiling beams from bowing.

keep – see bailey

king post – see roof timbers

linenfold – a pattern on wall panels imitating folded linen.

louvre – a covered turret above a medieval hall that allowed smoke to escape.

machicolation – see bailey

mannerism – see Artisan Mannerist

mansard – a roof with two separate pitches of slope.

motte – see bailey

mullion – central divider of window, made of metal or stone.

oversail – see jetty

oriel – an upper window projecting from a wall, sometimes (incorrectly) used to indicate a tall medieval window lighting the dais end of the Great Hall.

Palladian – a style of classical architecture, formal and refined outside, often lavish inside, named after Italian architect, Andrea Palladio (1508–80). Moving spirit behind most English classical designers, especially Inigo Jones and, later, Lord Burlington, William Kent and the early Georgians.

parlour – see solar

piano nobile – the main ceremonial floor of a classical building, sitting on the basement or 'rustic' lower floor.

pier-glass – a wall mirror supported by a small table, bracket or console.

pietra dura – literally 'hard stone'; a decorative inlay using highly polished stones such as marble, jasper and porphyry

pilaster – a flat column projecting only slightly from a wall.

pointing – mortar or cement used to seal between bricks.

porte-cochère – a grand porch with a driveway through it, allowing passengers to alight from carriages under cover.

prodigy house – a large, ostentatious house of the Elizabethan/Jacobean period.

putti – unwinged sculptures of chubby boys found in Classical and Baroque decoration.

queen post – see roof timbers

quoins – dressed corner stones.

render – a covering of stucco, cement or limewash on the outside of a building.

Rococo – the final phase of Baroque style in the 18th century, typified by refined painted and plaster decoration, often asymmetrical and with figures.

roof timbers – a tie-beam runs horizontally across the roof space; a king post rises vertically from the tie beam to the apex of the roof; queen posts rise not to the apex but to subsidiary beams known as collars; wind-braces strengthen the roof rafters.

rustic – a name given in Palladian architecture to the lower floor or basement, beneath the piano nobile.

rustication – treatment of ashlar by deep-cutting joints so they look stronger or cruder.

sashes – windows opening by rising on sash ropes or cords, as opposed to casements which open on side hinges.

scagliola – composition of artificial stone that imitates appearance of grained marble.

screens passage – accessed from the main door of a medieval building and built into one end of a Great Hall to shield it from draughts. Door ors arches lead from the passage into the hall on one side and kitchens on other. Above is usually a minstrels' gallery.

Serlian – motifs derived from pattern books of the Italian Renaissance architect, Sebastiano Serlio (1475–1554).

sgraffito – plaster decoration scratched to reveal another colour beneath.

solar – the upstairs room at the family end of a medieval hall, originally above an undercroft or parlour. Originally accessed by ladder or spiral stairs, it was usually replaced by a Great Chamber in the Tudor era.

strapwork – strap or ribbon-like decorative scrolls in Elizabethan and Jacobean design.

stucco – plaster, usually protective, covering for brick, sometimes fashioned to look like stone.

studding – vertical timbers laid close to each other to strengthen the wall. Close-studding tends to indicate wealth.

tie-beam – see roof timbers

undercroft – a vaulted room or crypt beneath a building, partly or wholly underground

vault – a ceiling, usually of stone composed of arches.

Venetian window – Palladian window composed of three components, the centre one arched.

wind-braces – see roof timbers

Simon Jenkins' sources

The best guides to any house are the people who occupy it. They have felt its walls and sensed its seasons. They stand witness to its ghosts, real and imagined, and have thus become part of its history. As a substitute, guidebooks vary widely from the academic to the plain childish. The best are published by English Heritage, erudite and enjoyable. National Trust guidebooks are at last moving from the scholarly to the accessible, and the Trust's compendium *Guide*, by Lydia Greeves and Michael Trinick, is excellent.

My selection of a thousand properties derives from numerous sources. These include Hudson's *Historic Houses and Gardens*, supplemented by *Museums and Galleries* published by Tomorrow's Guides. The Historic Houses Association website is another invaluable source. Of recent house surveys, the best are John Julius Norwich's *Architecture of Southern England* (1985), John Martin Robinson's *Architecture of Northern England* (1986) and Hugh Montgomery-Massingberd's *Great Houses of England and Wales* (2000). Nigel Nicolson's *Great Houses of Britain* (1978) describes the most prominent. Their lists are not exhaustive and include houses not open to the public. Behind them stands Nikolaus Pevsner's massive 'Buildings of England' series, which deals with houses more generously (with plans) in the newer revised editions.

On English domestic architecture, the classics are hard to beat. They include Olive Cook's *The English House Through Seven Centuries* (1968), Alec Clifton-Taylor's *The Pattern of English Building* (1972), Hugh Braun's *Old English Houses* (1962), Sacheverell Sitwell's *British Architects and Craftsmen* (1964) and Plantagenet Somerset Fry's *Castles of Britain and Ireland* (1980).

On specific periods the best are Mark Girouard's *Robert Smythson and the English Country House* (1983), Giles Worsley's *Classical Architecture in England* (1995), Kerry Downes's *English Baroque Architecture* (1966) and Girouard's *The Victorian Country House* (1971). Joe Mordaunt Crook takes a lively look at the Victorian battle of the styles in *The Dilemma of Style* (1989). Jeremy Musson describes the manorial revival in *The English Manor House* (1999) and Gavin Stamp takes a wider look at the same period in *The English House 1860–1914* (1986). *Edwardian Architecture*, edited by Alastair Service (1975), brings the story into the 20th century and Clive Aslet's *The Last Country Houses* (1982) almost completes it.

On social history, Girouard's *Life in the English Country House* (1978) is incomparable. *Creating Paradise* (2000) by Richard Wilson and Alan Mackley sets the house in its economic context. So does Mordaunt Crook's *The Rise of the Nouveaux Riches* (1999) and David Cannadine's *The Decline and Fall of the British Aristocracy* (1990). Adrian Tinniswood offers a fascinating insight in his *History of Country House Visiting* (1989). The desperate post-war bid to save houses is described in Marcus Binney's *Our Vanishing Heritage* (1984) and John Cornforth's *The Country Houses of England 1948–1998* (1998). Peter Mandler covers the same period in his scholarly *The Fall and Rise of the Stately Home* (1997).

Biographies of architects are too legion to list but Howard Colvin's *Biographical Dictionary of British Architects* (1978) was my bible over disputed dates and attributions. Of a more personal character is James Lees-Milne's delightful account of the National Trust's early acquisitions in *People and Places* (1992). Houses in distress are visited in John Harris's *No Voice from the Hall* (1998). *Writers and their Houses* (1993) is a first-class collection of essays, edited by Kate Marsh.

I am indebted to the many architectural commentaries in *Country Life*, champion of the historic buildings cause for over a century. I do not believe I could have found a thousand houses for my list were it not for its progenitors, Edward Hudson and Christopher Hussey, and their many successors.

Contact details

Note: Readers are advised to check opening times before visiting, either via the websites and addresses below or in Hudson's *Historic Houses & Gardens*, the annual guide to castles, houses and heritage sites open to the public.
Houses sited close to the border of a neighbouring county may have that county given as their postal address.

Adlington Hall – Macclesfield, Cheshire, SK10 4LF www.adlingtonhall.com Tel 01625 827595 Open Aug, Sun–Wed 2–5pm

Alton Castle – Catholic Youth Retreat Centre, Castle Hill, Alton, Staffordshire, ST10 4TT www.altoncastle.co.uk Tel 01538 703224 Contact the Retreat Centre for access information

Alton Towers – Alton, Staffordshire, ST10 4DB www.altontowers.com Tel 0870 4444455 Open mid-Mar–mid-Nov; opening hours vary, contact the theme park for further information

Arley Hall – Arley, Nr Northwich, Cheshire, CW9 6NA www.arleyhallandgardens.com Tel 01565 777353 Open Apr–Sep, Tue, Sun & BHs 12–5pm; gardens open Tue–Sun & BHs (also Sun only in Oct) 11am–5pm

Astley Hall – Astley Park, Chorley, Lancashire, PR7 1NP www.chorley.gov.uk/astleyhall Tel 01257 515555/515927 Open Apr–Oct, Fri–Sun 12–5pm and to pre-booked visits at other times

Barlborough Hall – Barlborough, Chesterfield, Derbyshire, S43 4TL Tel 01246 435138 Open during Easter, Whitsun and summer school holidays and at weekends by arrangement only

Barlaston Hall – Barlaston, Stoke-on-Trent, Staffordshire, ST12 9AT Tel 01782 372749 Open early Mar–mid-Sep, Tue 2–5pm

Beeston Castle – Chapel Lane, Beeston, Tarporley, Cheshire, CW6 9TX www.english-heritage.org.uk/beestoncastle Open all year, daily (Thur–Mon in Oct–Mar) 10am–6pm (to 4pm in Oct–Mar)

Belmont Hall – Great Budworth, Northwich, Cheshire, CW9 6HN Tel 01605 891235 Open during school holidays and at weekends for guided tours by arrangement only

Bolsover Castle – Castle Street, Bolsover, Derbyshire, S44 6PR www.english-heritage.org.uk/bolsover Tel 01246 822844 Open all year, Thur–Mon (May–Sep) 10am–5pm (to 4pm on Sat & in Nov–Mar, to 6pm in May–Sep)

Borwick Hall – Borwick, Carnforth, Lancashire, LA6 1JU Tel 01524 732508 Contact for access information

Bramall Hall – Bramhall Park, Stockport, Cheshire, SK7 3NX www.bramallhall.org.uk Tel 0845 833 0974 Open Apr–Dec, daily (Tue–Sun in Oct–Dec) 1–5pm (11am–4pm on BHs, 1–4pm on Fri–Sat and in Oct–Dec)

Browsholme Hall – Clitheroe, Lancashire, BB7 3DE www.browsholme.co.uk Tel 01254 827160 Open on certain days from Apr–Aug, 2–5pm, contact for further information; groups by arrangement during spring, summer and autumn

Burnley: Towneley Hall – Towneley Hall Art Gallery & Museums, Burnley, Lancashire, BB11 3RQ www.towneleyhall.org.uk Tel 01282 424213 Open Apr–Sat, Tue–Sun & BH Mon 11am–5pm (2–5pm on Sun)

Calke Abbey – Ticknall, Derbyshire, DE73 1LE www.nationaltrust.org.uk Tel 01332 863822 Open mid-Mar–late Oct, Sat–Wed 12.30–5pm

Capesthorne Hall – Siddington, Macclesfield, Cheshire, SK11 9JY www.capesthorne.com Tel 01625 861221 Apr–Oct, Sun, Mon & BHs 1.30–4pm

Carnfield Hall – South Normanton, Nr Alfreton, Derbyshire, DE55 2BE Tel 01773 520084 Open to groups by appointment

Casterne Hall – Ilam, Nr Ashbourne, Derbyshire, DE6 2BA www.casterne.co.uk Tel 01335 310489 Open early May–mid-Jun, Mon–Fri 2–4pm for tours on the hour

Catton Hall – Catton, Walton-on-Trent, Derbyshire, DE12 8LN www.catton-hall.com Tel 01283 716311 Open early Apr–mid-Oct, Mon at 2pm for guided tours and by arrangement at other times

Chatsworth – Bakewell, Derbyshire, DE46 1PP www.chatsworth.org Tel 01246 582204/565300 Open mid-Mar–late Dec, daily 11am–4.30pm; park open daily all year

Chesterfield: Revolution House – High Street, Old Whittington, Chesterfield, Derbyshire, S41 9JZ www.chesterfield.gov.uk Tel 01246 453554 Open late Mar–late Sep, Wed–Mon 11am–4pm

Chillington Hall – Codsall Wood, Wolverhampton, Staffordshire, WV8 1RE www.chillingtonhall.co.uk Tel 01902 850236 Open Easter–late May, Sun & BH Mons; July, Sun; Aug, Wed–Fri, Sun & BH Mon; 2–5pm

Cholmondeley Castle – Malpas, Cheshire, SY14 8AH Tel 01829 720383 Open Apr–Sep, Wed–Thur, Sun & BHs 11.30am–5pm

Clifton Hall – Clifton Campville, Staffordshire, B79 0BE Tel 01827 373681 Open by prior arrangement, all year, Mon–Fri 9am–5pm

Combermere Abbey – Whitchurch, Shropshire, SY13 4AJ www.combermereabbey.co.uk Tel 01948 662880 Open mid-Apr–early Jun, Wed–Thur for pre-booked tours only

Crewe Hall Hotel – Weston Road, Crewe, Cheshire, CW1 6UZ Tel 01270 253333

Croxteth Hall – Liverpool, Merseyside, L12 0HB www.croxteth.co.uk Tel 0151 233 6910 Open Easter–Sep, daily 10.30am–5pm; park open all year

Derby: Pickford's House – 41 Friar Gate, Derby, Derbyshire, DE1 1DA www.derby.gov.uk/museums Tel 01332 255363 Open all year, daily 10am–5pm (from 11am on Mon & 1–4pm on Sun & BHs)

Dorfold Hall – Acton, Nr Nantwich, Cheshire, CW5 8LD Tel 01270 625245 Open Apr–Oct, Tue & BH Mon 2–5pm

Dunham Massey – Altrincham Cheshire, WA14 4SJ www.nationaltrust.org.uk Tel 0161 941 1025 Open mid-Mar–late Oct, Sat–Wed 12–5pm (11am on BHs)

Eyam Hall – Eyam, Hope Valley, Derbyshire, S32 5QW www.eyamhall.com Tel 01433 631976 Open Easter week & Jul–Aug, Wed–Thur, Sun & BH Mon 12–4pm

Ford Green Hall – Ford Green Road, Smallthorne, Stoke-on-Trent, Staffordshire, ST6 1NG www.stoke.gov.uk/museums Tel 01782 233195 Open all year, Sun–Thur 1–5pm

Gawsworth Hall – Macclesfield, Cheshire, SK11 9RN www.gawsworthhall.com Tel 01260 223456 Open Easter & early May–late Sep, Sun–Wed (daily in Jul–Aug) 2–5pm

Gawthorpe Hall – Padiham, Nr Burnley, Lancashire, BB12 8UA www.nationaltrust.org.uk Tel 01282 771004 Open early Apr–late Oct, Tue–Thur & Sat–Sun (also Good Fri & BH Mon) 1–5pm; garden open all year, 10am–6pm

Haddon Hall – Bakewell, Derbyshire, DE45 1LA www.haddonhall.co.uk Tel 01629 812855 Open Easter–Oct, Sat–Mon (daily in May–Sep) 12–5pm

Haigh Hall – Haigh, Wigan, Lancashire, WN2 1PE Tel 01942 832895 Contact for access information

Hall i' th' Wood – Green Way, off Crompton Way, Bolton, Lancashire, BL1 8UA Tel 01204 332370 Open all year, Wed–Sun (Sat–Sun only in Nov–Mar) 11am–5pm

Hardwick Hall – Doe Lea, Chesterfield, Derbyshire, S44 5QJ www.nationaltrust.org.uk Tel 01246 850430 Open mid-Mar–late Oct, Wed, Thur, Sat, Sun, BH Mon & Good Fri 12–4.30pm

Hardwick Old Hall – Doe Lea, Chesterfield, Derbyshire, S44 5QJ www.english-heritage.org.uk/hardwick Tel 01246 850431 Open Apr–Oct, Wed, Thur, Sat, Sun 10am–6pm (to 5pm in Oct)

Heaton Hall – Heaton Park, Prestwich, Manchester, M25 2SW www.heatonpark.org.uk Tel 0161 773 1085 Open early Apr–late Sep, Wed–Sun & BH Mon 11am–5.30pm; park open all year, daily 8am–dusk

Highfields – Audlem, Nr Crewe, Cheshire, CW3 0DT Tel 01630 655479 Open for guided tours by prior written arrangement

Hoar Cross Hall Hotel – Yoxall, Lichfield, Staffordshire, DE13 8QS Tel 01283 575671

Hoghton Tower – Hoghton, Preston, Lancashire, PR5 0SH www.hoghtontower.co.uk Tel 01254 852986 Open Jul–Sep, Mon–Thur (also BH Sun & Mon through year excluding Christmas & New Year) 11am–4pm (1–5pm on Sun)

Ince Blundell – Ince Blundell Hall Nursing Home, Ince Blundell, Liverpool, Merseyside L38 6JL Tel 0151 929 2596 Contact for access information

Izaak Walton's Cottage – Worston Lane, Shallowford, Nr Stafford, Staffordshire, ST15 0PA www.staffordbc.gov.uk/heritage Tel 01785 760278 Open May–Aug, Sat–Sun 1–5pm

Kedleston Hall – Derby, Derbyshire, DE22 5JH www.nationaltrust.org.uk Tel 01332 842191 Open mid-Mar–late Oct, Sat–Wed (also Good Fri) 12–4.30pm

Kinver Rock Houses – Comber Road, Kinver, Nr Stourbridge, Staffordshire, DY7 6HU www.nationaltrust.org.uk Tel 01384 872553 Open early Mar–late Nov, Sat–Sun 2–4pm and for guided tours by prior arrangement at other times; grounds open early Apr–late Feb, daily 9am–7pm (to 4pm in early Oct–late Feb)

Lancaster: Cottage Museum – 15 Castle Hill, Lancaster, Lancashire, LA1 1YS Tel 01524 64637 Open Easter–Sep, daily 2–5pm

Lancaster : Judges' Lodgings – Church Street, Lancaster, Lancashire, LA1 1YS Tel 01524 32808 Open early Apr–late October, daily 1–4pm (from 12pm on Sat–Sun, and from 10am Mon–Fri in Jul–Sep)

Leighton Hall – Carnforth, Lancashire, LA5 9ST www.leightonhall.co.uk
Tel 01524 734474 Open May–Sep, Tue–Fri & BH Sun & Mon (all Sun in Aug)
2–5pm (from 12.30pm in Aug)

Lichfield: Erasmus Darwin House – Beacon Street, Lichfield, Staffordshire,
WA13 7AD www.erasmusdarwin.org Tel 01543 306260 All year, Tue–Sun
12–5pm

Lichfield: Johnson's Birthplace – Breadmarket Street, Lichfield,
Staffordshire, WS13 6LG www.lichfield.gov.uk/sjmuseum Tel 01543 264972
Open all year, daily 10.30am–4.30pm (from 12pm in Oct–Mar)

Little Moreton Hall – Congleton, Cheshire, CW12 4SD
www.nationaltrust.org.uk Tel 01260 272018 Open ealy Mar–mid-Dec, Wed–Sun
(& BH Mon in late Mar–early Nov, Sat–Sun only in early Nov–mid-Dec)
11.30am–5pm (to 4pm in early–mid-Mar & early Nov–mid-Dec)

Liverpool: Lennon House – Mendips, Melrose Avenue, Woolton, Liverpool,
Merseyside www.nationaltrust.org.uk Tel 0870 900 0256 Open for guided tours
only (with McCartney House, book in advance), late Mar–late Oct, Wed–Sun

Liverpool: McCartney House – 20, Forthlin Road, Liverpool, Merseyside
www.nationaltrust.org.uk Tel 0870 900 0256 Open for guided tours only (with
Lennon House, book in advance), late Mar–late Oct, Wed–Sun

Liverpool: Sudley House – Mossley Hill Road, Aigburth, Liverpool,
Merseyside, L18 8BX www.liverpoolmuseums.org.uk/sudley Tel 0151 724 3245
Open all year, daily, 10am–5pm

Lyme Park – Disley, Stockport, Cheshire, SK12 2NX www.nationaltrust.org.uk
Tel 01663 762023 Open late Mar–late Oct, Fri–Tue 1–5pm (from 11am on Good
Fri & BH Mons); gardens also open weekends early–late Mar & early Nov–mid-
Dec; park open all year, daily

Lytham Hall – Ballam Road, Lytham, Lancashire, FY8 4LE www.lythamhall.org
Tel 01253 736652 Open for guided tours, contact about tours and open days

Martholme – Great Harwood, Blackburn, Lancashire, BB6 7UJ
Tel 01254 886463 Open on certain days from spring to summer for tours at 2pm
& 4pm, contact for further information

Melbourne Hall – Melbourne, Derbyshire, DE73 8EN
www.melbournehall.com Tel 01332 862502 Open Aug, Tue–Sun & BH Mon
2–5pm; upstairs rooms by appointment only

Meols Hall – Churchtown, Southport, Merseyside, PR9 7LZ
www.meolshall.com Tel 01704 228326 Open mid-Aug–mid-Sep, daily 2–5pm

Moseley Old Hall – Fordhouses, Wolverhampton, Staffordshire, WV10 7HY
www.nationaltrust.org.uk Tel 01902 782808 Open early Mar–late Oct, Sat–Sun,
Wed, BH Mon & following Tue 12–5pm (from 11am on BH Mon); also for guided
tours in early Nov–mid-Dec, 12–4pm

Peckforton Castle Hotel – Stone House Lane, Peckforton, Tarporley,
Cheshire, CW6 9TN www.peckfortoncastle.co.uk Tel 01829 260930

Peover Hall – Over Peover, Knutsford, Cheshire, WA16 9HW
Tel 01565 632358 Open Apr–Oct, Mon (except BH Mon, stables & gardens also
open on Thur) 2–5pm

Quarry Bank Mill: The Apprentice House – Styal, Wilmslow, Cheshire,
SK9 4LA www.nationaltrust.org.uk Tel 01625 527468 Open mid-Mar–late Feb,
Tue–Sun (Wed–Sun in early Oct–late Feb) 12.30–4.30pm (from 11.30am in school
holidays); Quarry Bank Mill also daily mid-Mar–early Oct

Renishaw Hall – Sheffield, Derbyshire, S21 3WB www.sitwell.co.uk
Tel 01246 432310 Open for pre-booked tours only; gardens open Mar–Oct,
Thur–Sun & BHs 10.30am–4.30pm

Rode Hall – Church Lane, Scholar Green, Cheshire, ST7 3QP
www.rodehall.co.uk Tel 01270 873237 Open early Apr–late Sep, Wed & BHs by
arrangement

Rufford Old Hall – Rufford, Nr Ormskirk, Lancashire, L40 1SG
www.nationaltrust.org.uk Tel 01704 821254 Open late Mar–late Oct, Mon–Wed
& Sat–Sun 1–5pm

Salford: Ordsall Hall – Ordsall Lane, Salford, Manchester, M5 3AN
www.salford.gov.uk/ordsallhall Tel 0161 872 0251 Open all year, Sun–Fri (closed
Good Fri & Easter Sun) 10am–4pm (from 1pm on Sun)

Samlesbury Hall – Preston New Road, Samlesbury, Preston, Lancashire,
PR5 0UP Tel 01254 812010 Open all year, Sun–Fri 11am–4.30pm

Sandon Hall – Sandon, Staffordshire, ST18 0BZ www.sandonhall.co.uk
Tel 01889 508004 Open all year for pre-booked tours

Scarisbrick Hall – Kingswood College, Southport Road, Scarisbrick, near
Ormskirk, Lancashire L40 9RQ www.kingswoodcollege.co.uk Tel 01704 880200
Contact the school for access information

Shugborough – Milford, Staffordshire, ST17 0XB www.shugborough.org.uk &
www.nationaltrust.org.uk Open mid-Mar–late Oct, daily 11am–5pm

Sinai House – Shobnall Road, Burton-upon-Trent, Staffordshire, DE14 2BB
Tel 01283 544161/840732 Open by prior arrangement

Smithills Hall – Smithills Dean Road, Bolton, Lancashire, BL7 7NP
Tel 01204 332377 Open Apr–Sep, Tue–Sun & BH Mon 11am–5pm (2pm on Sun)

Speke Hall – The Walk, Liverpool, Merseyside, L24 1XD
www.nationaltrust.org.uk Tel 0151 427 7231 Open mid-Mar–early Dec,
Wed–Sun & BH Mon (Sat–Sun only early Nov–early Dec) 1–5pm (to 4.30pm in
early Nov–early Dec); grounds open all year, daily 11am–5.30pm

Stafford: Ancient High House – Greengate Street, Stafford, Staffordshire,
ST16 2JA www.staffordbc.gov.uk/heritage Tel 01785 619131 Open all year,
Tue–Sat 10am–4pm

Stonyhurst – Stonyhurst College, Stonyhurst, Clitheroe, Lancashire, BB7 9PZ
www.stonyhurst.ac.uk Tel 01254 826345 Open late Jul–late Aug, Sat–Thur
1–5pm

Sudbury Hall – Sudbury, Ashbourne, Derbyshire, DE6 5HT
www.nationaltrust.org.uk Tel 01283 585305/585337 Open mid-Mar–late Oct,
Wed–Sun & BH Mon 1–5pm

Sutton Scarsdale Hall – Hall Drive, Sutton Scarsdale, Chesterfield,
Derbyshire, S44 5UR www.english-heritage.org.uk/suttonscarsdale
Tel 01604 735400 (regional office) Open all year, 10am–6pm (to 4pm in winter)

Tabley House – Knutsford, Cheshire, WA16 0HB www.tableyhouse.co.uk
Tel 01565 750151 Open Apr–Oct, Thur–Sun & BHs 2–5pm

Tamworth Castle – The Holloway, Tamworth, Staffordshire, B79 7NA
www.tamworthcastle.co.uk Tel 01827 709626/709629 Open all year, Tue–Sun
(Thur–Sun in Nov–Mar) 12–5pm

Tatton Park & Old Hall – Knutsford, Cheshire, WA16 6QN
www.tattonpark.org.uk & www.nationaltrust.org.uk Tel 01625 534400
Open late Mar–early Sep; House open Tue–Sun & BH Mon 1–5pm, Old Hall open
Sat–Sun & BH Mon 12–5pm for tours only. Special openings for both during
school holidays

Tissington Hall – Ashbourne, Derbyshire, DE6 1RA www.tissington-hall.com
Tel 01335 352200 Open Easter & Whitsun BH weekend, then late Jul–late Aug,
Tue–Fri 1.30–4pm

Trentham Park – Stone Road, Trentham, Staffordshire, ST4 8AX
www.trentham.co.uk Tel 01782 646646 Gardens open all year, daily 10am–6pm
(to 4pm in Oct–Mar)

Turton Tower – Tower Drive, Chapeltown, Turton, Lancashire, BL7 0HG
Tel 01204 852203 Open Mar–Oct, Sat–Wed (Sat–Thur in May–Sep) 12–4pm (to
5pm in May–Sep)

West Bromwich: Oak House – Oak Road, West Bromwich, West Midlands,
B70 8HJ www.oakhouse.sandwell.gov.uk Tel 0121 553 0759 Open all year,
Tue–Fri & Sun (closed Sun in Oct–Mar) 10am–5pm (from 2pm on Sun)

West Bromwich: Old Manor House – Hall Green Road, West Bromwich,
West Midlands, B71 2EA Tel 0121 588 2035 Contact the public house for
opening information

Weston Park – Weston-under-Lizard, Nr Shifnal, Shropshire, TF11 8LE
www.weston-park.com Tel 01952 852100 Open Easter–early Sept, weekends &
BHs (daily in Jul–Aug, though may be closed for events) 1–5pm (grounds open
11am–6.30pm)

Whitmore Hall – Whitmore, Newcastle-under-Lyme, Staffordshire, ST5 5HW
Tel 01782 680478 Open May–Aug, Tue–Wed 2–5pm

Wightwick Manor – Wightwick Bank, Wolverhampton, West Midlands,
WV6 8EE www.nationaltrust.org.uk Tel 01902 761400 Open early Mar–late
Dec, Thur–Sat (also Wed & BH Sun & Mon in Aug) 12.30–5pm

Wingfield Manor – South Wingfield, Derbyshire, DE55 7NH
www.english-heritage.org.uk/wingfield Tel 01246 856456/857436 Open
Apr–Sep for pre-booked guided tours only on first Sat of the month

Winnington Hall – Winnington, Northwich, Cheshire, CW8 4DU
www.winningtonhall.co.uk Tel 01606 784171 Contact for visiting information

Wolverhampton: Bantock House – Finchfield Road, Wolverhampton,
West Midlands, WV3 9LQ www.wolverhamptonart.org.uk/bantock
Tel 01902 552195 Open all year, Tue–Sun 11am–5pm (12–4pm in Nov–Mar)

Wythenshawe Hall – Wythenshawe Park, Northenden, Manchester, M23 0AB
www.manchestergalleries.org Tel 0161 998 5083 Open early Jun–late Sep, Sat
11am–5pm

Index

Main entries for houses are in **bold**

Discover Britain's Historic Houses: Northwest England
Reader's Digest Project Team
Series editor Christine Noble
Project editor Lisa Thomas
Art editor Jane McKenna
Picture researcher Christine Hinze
Caption writer/copy editor Caroline Smith
Proofreader Ron Pankhurst
Indexer Marie Lorimer
Product production manager Claudette Bramble
Production controller Katherine Bunn

Reader's Digest General Books
Editorial director Julian Browne
Art director Anne-Marie Bulat
Managing editor Nina Hathway
Picture resource manager Sarah Stewart-Richardson
Pre-press account manager Penelope Grose

Colour origination Colour Systems Limited, London
Printed and bound in Europe by Arvato Iberia

We are committed to both the quality of our products and the service we provide to our customers. We value your comments, so please feel free to contact us on **08705 113366** or via our web site at **www.readersdigest.co.uk**

If you have any comments or suggestions about the content of our books, you can contact us at:
gbeditorial@readersdigest.co.uk

Published by The Reader's Digest Association Limited, 11 Westferry Circus, Canary Wharf, London E14 4HE

© The Reader's Digest Association Limited 2007

www.readersdigest.co.uk

® Reader's Digest, The Digest and the Pegasus logo are registered trademarks of the Reader's Digest Association, Inc., of Pleasantville, New York, USA.

This book was designed, edited and produced by The Reader's Digest Association Limited based on material from *England's Thousand Best Houses* by Simon Jenkins, first published by Allen Lane, the Penguin Press, a publishing division of Penguin Books Ltd.

Copyright © Simon Jenkins 2003

Concept code UK0149/L/S
Book code 634-009 UP0000-1
ISBN 978 0 276 44345 9
Oracle code 356600009H.00.24